Advance Praise for **RIDING SHOTGUN: THE ROLE OF THE COO**

What makes for a successful relationship between the CEO and the chief operating officer? Why do there seem to be so many examples where it just doesn't work as intended? Miles and Bennett offer well-thought-through perspectives on the factors which influence the success or failure of the chief operating officer role in today's corporation, supported by candid interviews with a number of well-known leaders. The result is a highly readable book which will help those considering creating such a role to go into it with their eyes wide open.

    —**LUCIEN ALZIARI,** Senior Vice President, Human Resources, Avon Products, Inc.

Under a weak CEO, the job is nothing short of agony. Under a great CEO, the COO's job is the best in the world—grounded in execution and performance metrics.

    —**PAULA ROSPUT REYNOLDS,** President and Chief Executive Officer, Safeco Corp.

Miles & Bennett tackle an important, and drastically under-researched area: the role, personalities, fit and success factors of COOs. We've seen several COOs who have been total winners, but it's striking how different the models of success can be depending on role, personal competencies, business situation/cycle/type, team strengths, and CEO strengths. The authors have done a very nice job of tying all of this together.

    —**JIM WILLIAMS,** Partner, Texas Pacific Group

The lessons reported in this book will be very useful to Boards, Heads of Human Resources, and CEOs as they consider succession planning and organizational design.

    —**DALE MORRISON,** President & Chief Executive Officer, McCain Foods Limited

The job of COO is becoming more important as companies and their boards look internally for succession alternatives. One question they face: Will the organization continue to run as the number 2 becomes the number 1? *Riding Shotgun* will help answer this and many more questions about the COO role in today's corporate structure.

    —**JOHN BERISFORD,** Senior Vice President, Human Resources,
      The Pepsi Bottling Group

The COO plays a critical leadership role in most businesses, but it's particularly true in the natural resources industry. Getting the right person on board and making sure that they are set up for success is critical. The information presented in this book is long overdue and will certainly help CEOs and Boards successfully design and implement the COO position.

    —**CHARLES (CHIP) GOODYEAR,** Chief Executive Officer, BHP Billiton

With the recent emphasis on enterprise performance and CEO succession planning, this book is a must-read for board members and executives who want to drive leadership capability and ensure sustained performance in their companies.

    —**CARLOS CARDOSO,** Chief Executive, Kennametal Inc.

RIDING SHOTGUN

The Role of the COO

NATHAN BENNETT AND

STEPHEN A. MILES

STANFORD BUSINESS BOOKS

An Imprint of Stanford University Press
Stanford, California

Stanford University Press
Stanford, California

Printed in the United States of America on acid-free, archival-quality paper

Library of Congress Cataloging-in-Publication Data

Bennett, Nathan, date-
  Riding shotgun : the role of the COO / Nathan Bennett and Stephen A. Miles.
    p. cm.
  Includes index.
  ISBN 0-8047-5166-8 (cloth : alk. paper)
  1. Chief operating officers. 2. Executive ability. 3. Leadership. 4. Management.
I. Miles, Stephen A. II. Title.
  HD38.2.B46218 2006
  658.4--dc22   2006004888

Original Printing 2006

Last figure below indicates year of this printing:

15   14   13   12   11

Typeset by Bruce Lundquist in 10.5/15 Minion

Special discounts for bulk quantities of Stanford Business Books are available to
corporations, professional associations, and other organizations. For details and
discount information, contact the special sales department of Stanford University
Press. Tel: (650) 736-1783, Fax: (650) 736-1784

CONTENTS

ACKNOWLEDGMENTS

We would like to acknowledge those individuals whose help was instrumental in bringing this work to fruition. We thank John Thompson and Joie Gregor, vice chairmen at Heidrick and Struggles, for making many of the introductions that led to executive interviews. Similarly, we thank Ginger Kent for making a number of additional introductions on our behalf. At Georgia Tech, a number of students played an important role by providing background research and by challenging our thinking as the project took shape: Kelly Dyar, Jeff Morton, Evan Gibson, J. P. Seriani, and Mike Orndorff. Second, we would like to thank Jason Daumeyer, engagement manager, and J. Hewins, principal in leadership consulting with Heidrick and Struggles, for their thorough work in researching and drafting the case studies that appear herein, as well as Rich Rosen and Fred Adair, partners in leadership consulting with Heidrick and Struggles. We also want to extend thanks to Mary Wedel at Heidrick and Struggles Leadership Consulting, who performed the most challenging tasks: scheduling the interviews and managing the transcription process. Finally, we would like to thank the executives who were so gracious in giving us their time to offer insights about the COO role so we could share them with you. We wish to thank those who preferred that we keep their contributions confidential and those named below:

Carol Bartz, Autodesk

John Brock, Former CEO of InBev and COO of Cadbury Schweppes

Jim Donald, Starbucks

Ken Freeman, Kohlberg Kravis Roberts & Co.

Robert Herbold, Herbold Group, former COO of Microsoft Corporation

Lois Juliber, Retired vice chairman, formerly COO of Colgate-Palmolive

Ray Lane, Kleiner Perkins Caufield and Byers, former COO of Oracle

Mike Lawrie, Formerly of Siebel Systems and IBM

Joe Leonard, AirTran

Shantanu Narayen, Adobe Systems

Bill Nuti, NCR, former COO and CEO of Symbol Technologies

Vincent Perro, Heidrick and Struggles Leadership Consulting

Fred Poses, American Standard Companies, former COO of Allied Signal

Steve Reinemund, PepsiCo, former COO of PepsiCo

Dan Rosensweig, Yahoo!

Kevin Sharer, Amgen, former COO of Amgen

Bruce Stein, The Hatchery, former COO of Mattel

William Swanson, Raytheon, former president of Raytheon

Mort Topfer, Castletop Capital, former vice chairman of Dell Inc.

Andrew Waitman, Celtic House

Craig Weatherup, Starbucks, former COO of Pepsi Bottling Group

Maynard Webb, COO, eBay

Wendall Weeks, Corning, former COO of Corning

Charles Wilson, Marks and Spencer

Del Yocam, Consultant, former COO of Apple Computer

Ed Zander, Motorola, former COO of Sun Microsystems

PREFACE

There are a dizzying number of books about leadership in organizations, and many more are produced each year. As of this writing, a keyword search for *leadership* on amazon.com yields more than 16,000 titles. A keyword search on *CEO* at that same site turns up just shy of 3,000 titles. Curiously, the search for CEO prompts the Website's database management software to query as to whether you really intended to search for CFO. We hadn't, but since the offer was made we gave it a shot. That search returned 239 titles—certainly a number that pales in comparison to 16,000 or 3,000.

We then tested the search engine on the object of our attention, the second in command, the chief operating officer. This search succinctly exemplifies the opportunity we saw for writing this book. The returns of the search consisted of a digital download of an article titled "Who Needs a COO?" (by Stuart Crainer); Okamoto condoms, in various packages; a VHS recording of a short film, "Bill and Coo"; an automotive crescent wrench; and a doll that "giggles and coos." Perhaps, we thought, the abbreviation has not made it into the business lexicon—or, more likely, it simply lacks the specificity required for an effective search. Searching on *chief operating officer,* however, returns only slightly more: the well-done book by David Heenan and Warren Bennis, *Co-Leaders: The Power of Great Partnerships,* and downloads of articles and announcements about COOs produced by Association Management, a publication of the American Society of Association Executives.

Though not quite as dramatic in proportion, Google results portray a similar pattern. Googling *chief executive officer* returned 35.4 million hits; *chief financial officer* yielded 23.3 million; and *chief operating officer* produced 14.9 million matches.

These "pop culture" indicators are simply two of many ways to support our contention that the COO role has not received sufficient attention. As the number two executive, the role is clearly important, but it is also highly complex and not well understood. In fact, some have argued that the number two position is "the toughest job in a company."[1] The COO is typically the key individual responsible for delivery of results day-to-day, quarter-to-quarter. The COO plays a critical leadership role in executing the strategies developed by the top management team. In many cases, COOs are groomed to be—or are actually being tested as—the organization's CEO-elect. Even if the effort has not been made to groom the successor, it may have been assumed. As Jay Conger and David Nadler note,

> When a CEO fails to prepare a potential successor and is suddenly pressured to step down, unexpectedly falls ill or passes away, it is not uncommon for the board to select the company's number-two executive by default. The appeal of the choice is quite simple: The second in command has likely played an instrumental role in the CEO's success and is well versed in the company's challenges.[2]

Further, several recent and very visible CEO appointments were a promotion of the second in command. To this point, the early returns suggest that individuals following this path, notably Sam Palmisano (IBM), Bill Swanson (Raytheon), Kevin Sharer (Amgen), and Kevin Rollins (Dell Computer), can be successful. As we elaborate herein, the role itself has unique characteristics that are largely due to idiosyncrasies of the business, its industry, and the CEO. Finally, the small bit of scholarly research focused on the COO role offers a quite counterintuitive finding: organizations with a COO perform more poorly than those without.

Together, these factors suggest that what is warranted is some systematic effort to better understand the role, when it makes sense for a company to create such a role, how to best staff the position (from inside or outside the company, with an individual possessing what sort of capability, and so on), and how an incumbent might be advised to enact the position. This is our purpose. Because there has not been a great deal of study of the position, we chose to rely heavily on interviews with executives who have served as COO and others who have elected—as CEO—either to create a COO role or *not* create a COO role. In addition, we interviewed search consultants who have experience helping organizations identify and attract individuals to the COO position. It is our hope that this approach results in a readable treatment of the topic and, more important, that the frameworks presented herein form a basis for future effort that helps in understanding the role of the COO.

Nathan Bennett

Stephen A. Miles

Atlanta, Georgia

September 2005

NOTES

1. Robert Lear, quoted in Ettore, B. February 1993. Who is this person: Focus on the number two. *Management Review*.
2. Conger, J. A., and Nadler, D. A. 2004. When CEOs step up to fail. *Sloan Management Review*, 45(3).

RIDING SHOTGUN

1

INTRODUCTION

Without a second fiddler, there's no orchestra.
Robert Hodgson[1]

This book offers systematic examination of an increasingly critical role in organizations: that of the chief operating officer. Whereas a substantial body of literature focuses on leadership and chief executive officers, written by academics (e.g., *The Leadership Challenge*, by James Kouzes and Barry Posner; *Bad Leadership*, by Barbara Kellerman; *Good to Great: Why Some Companies Make the Leap and Others Don't*, by Jim Collins), consultants (e.g., *The Leadership Wheel*, by C. Clinton Sidle), and practitioners (e.g., *Winning*, by Jack Welch; *Iacocca: An Autobiography*, by Lee Iacocca; *Leadership*, by Rudy Giuliani; *The Source of Success: The Five Enduring Principles at the Heart of Real Leadership*, by Peter Georgescu; and *Authentic Leadership*, by Bill George), there is a dearth of work that focuses on the role of the number two—a role we think is of particular interest because in those companies where the position exists the incumbent is such a visible and important leader *and* follower.

COOs occupy a position that is unique structurally, strategically, socially, and politically. As a result, many of the challenges faced by incumbents are also unique (e.g., managing the relationship with the CEO and other company leaders, implementing the directions of the CEO). Because the role has not received much attention, we know very little about the reasons behind its creation, how it is enacted in various organizations and shaped by incumbents, or the requisite characteristics of a successful COO. In the following chapters we (1) clearly articulate the unique characteristics of the COO role, (2) describe the various motives for establishing a COO position, (3) review the challenges associated with successful performance of the COO role, and (4) develop a set of strategies or principles to inform individuals who aspire to serve in such a position some day.

To accomplish these purposes, we rely on a combination of first-person interviews with current and past COOs, case studies that describe various ways organizations have structured leadership with or without a COO role, reviews of the extant research and other writings on the COO role, and interviews with executive search professionals who have placed many high-profile COOs. Our typology demonstrates the breadth of motivation companies have for making the strategic decision to create a COO position. Additionally, we present the major barriers to success in the COO role and consideration of the knowledge, skills, and competencies associated with effective performance of the role. We also consider the areas that it is essential for a CEO to understand in successfully bringing on and then managing a COO, as well as the relationships that the COO must manage, especially those involving the CEO, the board, and other executives. In the end, we offer helpful insights to organizational decision makers confronted with decisions about when and how to create, structure, and staff a COO position, as well as to individuals considering or already occupying a COO role. In doing so, we aim to furnish important insights into the execution issues to which a board and top managers must attend in order to effectively implement this particular leadership configuration.

BACKGROUND

It is easily argued that the job of CEO has become increasingly demanding in recent years. The reasons driving this are many, but clearly macroeconomic factors such as the complexity of managing a globally competitive business and heightened public concern regarding issues such as corporate social responsibility and financial fraud play a major role. As a result of the pressure the CEO faces to manage relationships with myriad external constituents, many organizations have created a "second in command." Though the precise duties of this second in command, what we call the chief operating officer, vary considerably both from one organization to another and over time within a single firm, an overriding goal is to provide sufficient high-level support to the CEO.

In recent years, the COO has arguably become a more visible member of the top management team. At the same time, there has been little study of the role. Consequently, we do not know much about the organizational circumstances that support creation of a COO position, or about how to properly design the position. We also know little about how myriad contingencies such as environmental, firm, and individual characteristics might determine the precise configuration of roles and responsibilities to invest in a COO position. Just as we do not have a good understanding of the proper definition of the COO role, we do not know much about the knowledge, skills, abilities, competencies, and experiences that might predict the success of an individual in this role. The same applies to what life is like for the incumbent in the role, and the degree to which it prepares—or should prepare—an individual to ultimately serve an organization as a CEO. Finally, we must learn a great deal about how this CEO/COO structure affects organizational performance—does it lead to the results one would likely have sought through establishing the COO role? In fact, the scant research that does exist in this area suggests it may not.[2] In all, whether or not—or when—the designation of a second in command is a good model for leading organizations is an open question, as is how to structure and fill such a position. Our goal in this book is to begin the process of developing a systematic framework to help business leaders understand whether, when, and how to implement and fill a COO position.

THE COO ROLE

As CEOs are expected to spend more and more time outside their organizations, the COO has taken on more and more responsibility for the oversight of daily organizational operations. On the positive side, it can be argued that allowing the CEO to focus on strategic, longer-term challenges the company faces, and creating a role (that of the COO) to lend leadership and oversight to day-to-day company operations, improves the effectiveness of the individuals in both functions. Clearly, the position at the top has grown; to conclude that the responsibilities could be better addressed if divided makes intuitive sense. On the other hand, some have suggested that separating responsibility for strategy formulation from strategy implementation is a major mistake.[3] Further, in some dramatic examples CEOs have used what they would view as a necessary distance from day-to-day operations as an excuse that should protect them from responsibility for misdeeds and unethical or illegal behavior displayed by members of top management.[4] This so-called dummy defense is expected to play a key role in efforts on the part of some high-profile CEOs to avoid penalties for financial fraud that could include jail time: Walter Forbes (CUC International), whom the *New York Times* reported felt little need to attend to happenings inside the company; Richard Scrushy (HealthSouth); Bernard J. Ebbers (WorldCom); and Ken Lay and Jeffrey Skilling (Enron).[5] In fact, one consulting firm found that in 2002 only 17 percent of the companies that promoted the COO to CEO replaced the COO. The interpretation of the finding was that it gave evidence that investors want to force the CEO to stay close to the business.[6] In our interviews, we found that several new CEOs did not plan to immediately recruit a COO because they wanted to be close to the business. However, they also indicated that this model may not be sustainable in the long run and that, as they began to think about succession, the appropriateness of the role would likely reemerge.

In our interviews with executives, it quickly became clear that the most critical element in successfully implementing the role is a trusting relationship between the COO and the CEO. As Andrew Waitman said to us, at his company (Celtic House) there is an understanding that the COO (David Adderley) is the person you would want holding the rope, should you find yourself dangling off a cliff—your trust in the person and his or her capabilities is that strong. Charles Wilson, the executive director at Marks and Spencer Group, elaborated on this point in noting that the trust has to be about both personal integrity and competence. In the most positive case, what might be achieved is a productive work arrangement like that described by Heenan and Bennis in their recent book *Co-Leaders: The Power of Great Partnerships.*[7] This notion has been translated as "two in a box" and is explicitly practiced today by such businesses as Dell (Michael Dell and Kevin Rollins), Microsoft (Bill Gates and Steve Ballmer), and Synopsys (Aart de Geus and Chi-Foo Chan). If two in a box is viewed as the exemplar for leadership at the top of an organization, the other extreme is characterized best by Harry Levinson in a 1993 article; he directly addressed the particular challenges in creating a number two role, noting that:

The relationship between the chief executive officer and the chief operating officer in any organization is fraught with many psychological complexities. Perhaps it is the most difficult of all organizational working relationships because more than others, it is a balancing act on the threshold of power.[8]

The key ingredient for COO effectiveness is often whether the CEO is ready to share power. Unfortunately, some COOs do not realize the CEO is not ready until they are in the position and friction begins to appear in the relationship. We explore the theme throughout this book because clearly organizations must anticipate and avoid the dysfunction that can arise from a poor match between CEO and COO: unhealthy rivalry, defensiveness, overcontrol, rigidity, misconceptions, and doubt.[9]

Until quite recently, academic investigation typically focused only indirectly on COOs. Some explored the characteristics that help a COO become a successful CEO. That is, the research is designed to help predict COOs' performance in their next job, not the current one. A second thread of study explored this role through examining CEO succession.[10] An example of this research considers how COOs as "insiders" fare as CEO, compared to "outsiders." The third cluster of study looked at the COO role in special circumstances where the CEO and COO function as "co-leaders."[11] Most recently, Cannella and Hambrick investigated the factors associated with creating a COO position, as well as the relationship between the presence of a COO and organization performance. Cannella and Hambrick found the relationship to be negative; the presence of a COO was associated with a lower level of organizational performance.[12] This research was widely cited in practitioner publications (see, for example, *Industry Week*, April 2004), but without much effort to aid in understanding or explain the reason for the counterintuitive finding. Hambrick was quoted as suggesting that companies with COOs are at a disadvantage because either (1) the CEO-COO structure is an inferior one or (2) the presence of a COO is an indicator that the CEO is not capable. Whereas these are the more controversial among plausible explanations, it also clear that many alternative explanations may be salient. Perhaps the COO was a poor choice. Perhaps the effort to demarcate the CEO's work from that of the COO was muddled, poorly designed, or inadequately communicated and the resulting confusion led to poor decisions by members of the organization. Perhaps the efforts of the CEO to smoothly bring the COO on board were inadequate. Perhaps the plan was perfect but the implementation fell short.

In all, the fact that we do not know what makes the CEO-COO structure work suggests that more thought on the subject is warranted. So, although the Cannella and Hambrick study represents a start in an effort to understand the COO role, the fact remains that not much is known about how organizations might best structure the COO role—or, quite frankly, about how to select an effective COO. The prevalence of the role (in the last eighteen months, COO announcements have been made by companies in a range of industries, among them Time Warner, Microsoft, Radio Shack, Airbus, Allstate Insurance, KPMG, Alcatel, Chiron, Nissan Motor, BellSouth, Comcast, MetLife, Viacom, Ford, and Medtronic)[13], combined with general lack of understanding of the role, its context, and the factors associated with its successful execution lend an urgency to this work.

A TYPOLOGY OF COOS

As is the case with many issues, clear definition of the COO is an important place to start. In the broadest sense, this is not difficult: The COO is the second in command and has responsibility for day-to-day operations of a business. The definition is intuitive, but it can be difficult for an outsider to understand who holds this position; sometimes COO and sometimes another title is used to denote the role.

Further, when a reader is immersed in the literature to investigate this more closely, it quickly becomes apparent, even after solving the labeling challenge, that a COO is not a COO is not a COO. In some firms, the COO has a narrow mission to address a specific business need. For example, Microsoft filled Rick Belluzzo's position as COO with Kevin Turner from Wal-Mart after it had been vacant for several years. Turner is expected to use his retail experience to help Microsoft grow the consumer products business.[14] In other enterprises, the COO's role has been nearly that of a Zen master as mentor to a developing CEO. We have observed that the main driver behind the sometimes subtle and sometimes not-so-subtle differences among COO roles is the firm's motive in creating the position. Though these motives should not be viewed as being mutually exclusive, treating them as such makes for a more straightforward initial explanation. Our research identified seven motivations behind creation of the COO position:

1. To provide daily leadership in an *operationally intensive* business
2. To lead a specific *strategic imperative* undertaken by management, such as a turnaround, major organizational change, or planned rapid expansion, or to cope with a dynamic environment
3. To serve as a *mentor* to a young or inexperienced CEO (often a founder)
4. To *balance* or complement the strengths of the CEO
5. To foster a strong partnership at the top—the *two-in-a-box* model
6. To teach the business to the *heir apparent* to the current CEO
7. To *retain* executive talent that other firms may be pursuing, absent an imperative from the business for creating the position

We consider the first two situations—an operationally intensive business and a strategic imperative—to be *firm-focused* motivation. That is, the claim that the position serves to address a need of the firm has high face validity. The next three situations—COO as mentor, a balance to a CEO, or as part of a two-in-a-box partnership at the top of the organization—are what we consider *CEO-focused* motivation. In each instance, the CEO is the most direct beneficiary of the COO position. Finally, we consider cases where the COO position is created to retain talent or develop the heir apparent as *COO-focused* motivation. Here, the COO is the first beneficiary of the creation.

Examples of firms that appear to represent each motivation may serve to further explain the typology. First, the COO position is nearly ubiquitous in operationally intensive businesses such as the airline, disk drive, and automotive industries. For example, Seagate Technologies, an $8 billion vertically integrated manufacturer of disk drives, now operates with a CEO (Bill Watkins) and a COO (David Wickersham). Previously, Watkins served as the COO for then-CEO Steven Luczo. As this example illustrates, the complexity of managing a vertically integrated global manufacturing enterprise while simultaneously satisfying numerous external commitments placed on a CEO sometimes takes two sets of hands.

Second, organizations have identified individuals and placed them in the COO role as a change agent—with the specific instruction to redirect the company (e.g., a turnaround or radical change). Ray Lane and his work at Oracle serves as a good example of an executive brought in to lead a turnaround, initially for the most troubled geography (United States) and later for the broader organization as the president/COO. At the time of Lane's appointment, Oracle was flirting with bankruptcy and the organizational culture was dysfunctional. Larry Ellison hired Lane (not an obvious candidate) from Booz Allen and Hamilton. As Lane explains,

> My position at Oracle, as well as Jeff Henley's [CFO], was created in response to pressure from the Board on Larry Ellison due to the prior year's performance of Oracle. The Board had a concern: whereas Larry was a visionary leader, the company needed more discipline in its operations. To help along those lines, I was brought on board, as was Jeff Henley as CFO. From the beginning, Larry defined the three positions as "the Office of the CEO." Clearly, making this work depends heavily on shared understandings of who is responsible for what and on very effective communication among all involved.

Ellison brought him in initially as the president of U.S. Operations, to turn around the deeply troubled sales and marketing functions, which were running poorly. He was later named president and COO of the company and in that role contributed to a dramatic increase in stock price over ten years.

Another example is Joe Leonard, the chief executive officer of AirTran Airways, who recruited Robert ("Bob") Fornaro to be his COO and help him lead a dramatic turnaround. Leonard stated that the company was "running on fumes" and needed dramatic efforts to stave off bankruptcy. Similarly, organizations that operate in a hypercompetitive and dynamic marketplace, such as high technology, often choose to create a COO position. In this instance, the organization requires the number two to be maniacally focused on day-to-day execution, while the number one focuses on strategy and the future to ensure that they do not miss changes in the industry and technology. One is clearly oriented with its "head up" to understand success in the future, whereas the other is oriented "head down" into the operational details necessary for success today. This has worked at businesses such as Yahoo!, where CEO Terry Semel brought in Dan Rosensweig to serve as COO. In contrast, in February

2005 Carly Fiorina was forced out of her position as chairman and CEO by the Hewlett-Packard board, in some measure because she resisted the pressure to create a number two position.[15] Fiorina's reluctance to have a strong second chair led one individual to say that her hands-on style "slowed things down" for the company as it tried to compete against such strong players as IBM and Dell in a dynamic, fast-paced, and difficult industry.[16]

In the third case, the hiring of a COO provides some balance to the top management team—when the CEO demonstrates lack of deep experience or, perhaps surprisingly, lack of interest in particular aspects of his or her leadership role. For example, a company with a young CEO (such as the founder of a rapidly growing entrepreneurial venture) might seek a COO with experience and (ideally) wisdom that can develop both the CEO and the emerging business. One could logically hypothesize that as the CEO develops, the COO role might either disappear or be heavily restructured. Such was arguably the rationale for young Michael Dell's hiring Mort Topfer at Dell Inc.[17] Here, Topfer was initially recruited to simply be Dell's mentor. Dell's company had succeeded to a point where it could have begun to get ahead of his experience. Dell had sufficient self-awareness to acknowledge that he needed some "gray hair" and deep experience around to accelerate the company's growth as well as his development as a leader. Importantly, Topfer was fifty-eight years old at the time and was completing a successful career at Motorola. He clearly had no aspirations of becoming Dell's CEO; he was there to help Michael Dell. A second example is when Netscape founder Marc Andreessen recruited James Barksdale. Barksdale joined the company as president and chief executive officer and was able to be a mentor to the young founder and help him develop his leadership and managerial capabilities. Likewise, though he held the title of CEO, Eric Schmidt was recruited by Google to provide similar expertise and support for cofounders Larry Page and Sergey Brinn. We found clear designation of a second in command quite regularly in high-technology companies. As Ray Lane told us:

> Many high-technology firms are led by a CEO/founder. These CEOs began as technical or domain experts and as the firm has grown they have held on to the CEO title. For many of these people, their interest is the technology or the resulting products—not running an operation. They likely find the day-to-day

running of the company to be mundane—it just isn't what they wake up wanting to go and do. In those instances, the COO position allows them to continue to think about what they love, knowing that the company is being well led.

Fourth, it may be a matter of style or preference rather than experience that suggests what is in order is a COO who can complement a CEO. Observers have characterized the relationship between Bill Gates and a pair of his number twos, Jon Shirley and Michael Hallman, in such a light.[18] Observers noted that COO Shirley brought a "calm, self-effacing balance" to Gates.[19] In a case like this, there is no expectation that the COO role will lead to a higher position.

Fifth, consider the model where the CEO and COO operate as two in a box (what Heenan and Bennis termed co-leaders). Michael Dell and Kevin Rollins, whom Dell introduced as COO in 1996, are an example of this model. Both are committed to leading the company together, now as chairman (Dell) and CEO (Rollins). This desire is reflected in their decision to "co-office" as well; their offices are adjoined with only a glass partition between them. Some organizations have expanded the concept to three in a box: Nike and C-Span are two that established "co-presidents." Taking this concept a step further, Ellison at Oracle recently appointed a third co-president, Gregory Maffei, who joins Charles Phillips and Safra Catz in that role.

Sixth, the motivation may be to create a position that allows an heir apparent to assimilate—to learn the company, its business and environment, and its people. A recent example of a company using the COO position to develop the successor to the CEO job is Continental Airlines, where CEO Gordon Bethune (who originally joined the airline as its COO) announced that he is passing the torch to his COO, Larry Kellner.[20] Similarly, Ian Cook was named COO at Colgate-Palmolive, an announcement that was taken to indicate he was the likely successor to Reuben Mark, the long-time CEO.[21] In the time since Rex Tillerson's appointment to the number two position at Exxon, observers have noted that he was increasingly exposed to the public—a deliberate effort to facilitate his likely succession to CEO Lee Raymond.[22] Finally, Norfolk Southern announced appointment of Charles Moorman to its COO position, continuing the company's "practice of picking an executive young enough to lead the company for at least a decade."[23] Delta Air Lines went without a COO for some time before announcing in July 2005 that Jim Whitehurst, a possible successor to CEO Gerald Grinstein, would fill that position.[24] The highest-profile example of this strategy is arguably Lou Gerstner's decision to appoint Sam Palmisano as COO at IBM. Certainly, being identified as a likely heir does not represent a guarantee. A danger apparent in this strategy is the loss of the heir if ultimately the top job is not given over—or at least not given on schedule. In some cases, performance as COO indicates to the organization that the heir title was inappropriately or prematurely assigned to the candidate. In the past few years, COOs Steve Heyer (Coca-Cola), John Brock (Cadbury Schweppes), Mike Zafirovski (Motorola), John Walter (AT&T), Michael Ovitz (Disney), and Robert Willumstad (Citigroup) left their companies because they were passed over for the CEO position—realizing the timing for the succession was not as had been advertised—or left involuntarily.[25] Some CEOs have even gone so far as to create a structure that deliberately avoids a number two position. For example, Polaroid founder Edwin Land discussed his desire to make it clear there was not a second in command, saying, "There isn't any number two; there are lots of number threes."[26]

Where the role was created as a learning opportunity for the COO, the position may not outlast the tenure of its incumbent. In fact, there are instances where the incumbents work themselves out of the job. Such was the case at the Kauffman Foundation; COO Paul Carttar stepped down after one year when the foundation "decided to abolish the chief operating officer job" in an effort to streamline operations.[27]

Finally, in a number of cases creating the role of COO seems to be motivated as much by the presence of an individual with apparent skills as it is by a specific organizational need. That is, the role seems to be created to retain or attract talent more so than to address a particular organizational or leadership gap. For example, News Corp/Fox Entertainment recently announced that its president and COO, Peter Chernin, had signed a new employment agreement preventing a rumored move to rival Disney.[28] Similarly, McDonald's recently announced efforts to restructure its U.S. and Europe president positions, a move interpreted by analysts as an effort to ward off poachers.[29] As further evidence of the position's use to place a person, rather than meet a business imperative, we uncovered a number of instances where the position does not outlast its incumbent; when the COO leaves, the duties are "divided among top management" and the role disappears. For example, when Rick Belluzzo left Microsoft, the company kept the COO position vacant for several years before hiring Kevin Turner. When Steve Heyer left Coca-Cola, his duties were divided and the position was not filled. When Kevin Rollins was promoted to CEO with Dell, a new COO was not named. Finally, when COO Gary Daichendt left Nortel Networks (after just three months), his duties were assumed by the CEO, Bill Owens.[30] Or it may be that the role sits idle until the next heir is identified. Such has been the case at Intel, a business with a long history of deliberately managing succession. Since the time of Paul Otellini's promotion, no successor as COO has been named.[31]

It is important to note that any of these motivations for creating the COO position can be carried out well or poorly—efforts to understand the effectiveness of the COO position need to be sensitive to disentangling cause for performance that should be attributed to the COO's efforts, the structure itself, or a poor implementation. Whereas Donald Hambrick's suggestion that (1) the CEO-COO structure may be fatally flawed and (2) a COO is a signal of a weak CEO merits consideration, so do a range of less-dramatic but equally consequential possibilities. Broadly stated, it may be that an organization's motivation for and its implementation of a COO position, as well as its success in finding the right candidate, might be important contributors to subsequent company performance.

SUMMARY

The COO or second-in-command role continues to be practiced in organizations of various sizes and in a range of industries. The position is unique for a number of reasons. First is the diversity of roles the incumbent may play at various times in relationship to the CEO: loyal follower, leader of those charged with executing the business strategy, devil's advocate, strategic partner, mentor, heir, and so on. Second, the position is highly visible, particularly to internal audiences. As a result, ongoing alignment of the visions espoused by the CEO and COO is critical. Despite the role's prevalence and importance, it has not received much attention; as a result, many aspects of how it is best implemented are not well understood. In fact, the early evidence is that it may not be well done in many of the places where the position exists. Our purpose is to begin to construct a foundation from which we can better understand the role so that it can, in fact, be implemented in a way that brings benefit to chief executives, top management teams, incumbent COOs, and company stakeholders. Specifically, we are interested in helping to shape a better understanding of these interrelated questions:

- When does it make sense to create a COO role?
- How should the COO role take shape? How is the role best designed?
- What type of individual is best suited to serve as COO?

As is the case with many aspects of organizations, we do not anticipate a best answer to any of these questions. Rather, we hope that our efforts and the responses from the executives we interviewed give the reader the ability to understand how the particular circumstances faced by a single organization might influence how these questions should be framed, debated, and answered.

To begin this process, we identified a framework that elaborates seven motivations that organizations expressed—through our interviews or through media reports—for creating a COO role. One way to view this framework is to ask who is intended to be the primary beneficiary of the role: the firm, the CEO, or the new COO? We suggest that answering this question establishes a foundation for determining the best way to staff the COO role. Clearly, if the need is a mentor for the founder of an exploding business, the COO position and incumbent differ from what is needed for an heir apparent—someone ready to take the reigns in five years—or to find a perfect match to the CEO to execute a two-in-a-box structure. Understanding whether or not the COO role will lead to long-term benefits should begin with an understanding of these situational aspects of creating the role and identifying its incumbent, as well as understanding the success of the implementation and the incumbent's coming on board.

Next, we conducted interviews with more than two dozen executives, all of whom have considerable experience at or near the top of major corporations. Many are currently serving or have served as COOs. Others lead organizations; of those, some have COOs in place, whereas others have deliberately chosen not to adopt such a leadership structure. Some individuals have experience to share both from their time as a COO and now as a CEO with a COO on board. Though our respondents touch on a number of themes during the conversations that follow, there are some key points to watch for:

- The importance of the CEO and COO developing a shared understanding of where the other's job begins and ends
- The degree to which the COO enacts the role in a way that offers important help to the CEO, in contrast to the degree to which the presence of the COO creates a layer of insulation that actually keeps the CEO from thoroughly understanding the company
- The various ways to structure the role of the COO with the board
- The characteristics of a well-designed effort to bring on board a COO from outside the company
- The importance of trust as the foundational element of the CEO-COO relationship
- How both business need and interpersonal chemistry influence the right choice of COO
- The importance for the CEO to give the COO room to have his or her own voice at the company; the breadth of experience required to be successful as COO, as well as the relentlessness of the job
- The degree to which performance as a COO prepares one to be a CEO, as contrasted with the degree to which it labels one as a transactional, rather than strategic, manager
- The challenges faced by an outsider coming in to a COO role
- The critical nature of the COO's ability to drive strategy through the organization
- The importance for the COO to check ego at the door and sublimate concerns regarding assignment of credit and blame

Throughout the interviews, points of similarity and departure in their opinions are readily discerned. There are clearly areas in which consensus exists, as with the importance of clearly delineated boundaries between the jobs of CEO and COO and the role that trust, communication, and chemistry play in the success of the CEO-COO structure. At the same time, there are certainly areas where a range of perspectives exists, as with the life span of the typical COO (if there is such a thing) and the degree to which the role prepares its incumbent for the CEO position. We report herein our conversations with these individuals:

Ed Zander, chairman and CEO, Motorola

Carol Bartz, chairman, CEO, and president, Autodesk

John Brock, formerly CEO of InBev and COO of Cadbury Schweppes

Jim Donald, CEO, Starbucks

Ken Freeman, managing director, Kohlberg Kravis Roberts & Co.

Mike Lawrie, formerly CEO of Siebel Systems

Joe Leonard, chairman and CEO, AirTran Airways

Fred Poses, chairman and CEO, American Standard Companies

Steve Reinemund, chairman and CEO, PepsiCo

Kevin Sharer, CEO of Amgen

William Swanson, chairman and CEO, Raytheon

Craig Weatherup, director, Starbucks

Del Yocam, formerly COO of Apple Computer

Robert Herbold, formerly COO, Microsoft

Jim Donald, Starbucks

Shantanu Narayen, president and COO of Adobe Systems

Bill Nuti, CEO, NCR

Vincent Perro, formerly COO of Nextera Enterprises

Dan Rosensweig, COO, Yahoo!

Bruce Stein, formerly COO, Mattel

Mort Topfer, formerly COO of Dell Inc.

Maynard Webb, COO, eBay

Wendell Weeks, president and CEO, Corning

NOTES

1. http://www.forministry.com/Article.asp?Record=3184.

2. Hambrick, D. C., and A. A. Cannella, Jr. 2004. CEOs who have COOs: Contingency analysis of an unexplored structural form. *Strategic Management Journal*, 25, 959–980.

3. Donald Hambrick, in Guinto, J. 2004, August 15. Where did all the COOs go? *American Way*.

4. Norris, F. 2005, January 7. Chief executive was paid millions, and he never noticed the fraud? *New York Times*, Sect. C1.

5. Ibid.

6. Guinto (2004).

7. Heenan, D. A., and W. Bennis. 1999. *Co-Leaders: The power of great partnerships*. New York: Wiley.

8. Levinson, H. 1993. Between CEO and COO. *Academy of Management Executive*, 7, 71–81.

9. Ibid.

10. Cannella, A. A., and W. Shen. 2001. So close and yet so far: Promotion versus exit for CEO heirs apparent. *Academy of Management Journal*, 44, 252–270; Shen, W., and A. A. Cannella. 2002a. Power dynamics within top management and their impacts on CEO dismissal followed by inside succession. *Academy of Management Journal*, 45, 1195–1206; Shen, W., and A. A. Cannella. 2002b. Revisiting the performance consequences of CEO succession: The impacts of successor type, postsuccession senior executive turnover, and departing CEO tenure. *Academy of Management Journal*, 45, 717–733.

11. Heenan and Bennis (1999).

12. Hambrick and Cannella (2004).

13. Siklos, R. 2005, December 22. Time Warner chooses an insider as president. *New York Times*, Sect. C1; Guth, R. A., and A. Zimmerman. 2005, August 5. Microsoft picks a WalMart vet to be its no. 3. *Wall Street Journal*, Sect. B1; McDonald's exec named new COO at RadioShack. *Retail Merchandiser*, 2005, 45(8), 54; Flottau, J. 2005. Airbus reshuffles executive ranks: Promotes champion to COO. *Aviation Daily*, 361(13), 1; Cornejo, R. 2005. Allstate Corp names Wilson new president and COO. *Best's Review*, 106(3), 12; Flynn succeeds ailing chief, Veihmeyer becomes deputy. (2005, 9 June). *Wall Street Journal*; Quigley is appointed president and COO. (2005, April 20). *Wall Street Journal*; Chiron fills president, operating chief post. (2005, February 24). *Wall Street Journal*; Nissan Motor Corporation. (1995, February 24). *Wall Street Journal*; BellSouth names new COO. (2004, December 3). *Atlanta Business Chronicle*, Sect. A12; Key, P. 2004, July 9. Comcast picks Burke as COO. *Philadelphia Business Journal*; Henrikson is named president and COO. (2004, June 23). *Wall Street Journal*; Grego, M., and Lafayette, J. MTV: Making the heir cut. *TelevisionWeek*, June 7, 2004; Kerwin, K., and G. Edmondson. 2004, May 10. Will slow and steady win the race? As new COO, James Padilla has to keep the improvements coming. *BusinessWeek*; Burton, T. 2004, May 3. Medtronic set to name Hawkins as president, operating chief. *Wall Street Journal*, Sect. B5.

14. Jones, T. 2005, August 5. Microsoft finds a high-level exec at Wal-Mart. *Los Angeles Times*.

15. La Monica, P. R. 2005, February 9. Fiorina out, HP stock soars. *CNN Money*.

16. Tam, P.-W. 2005, January 24. Hewlett-Packard board considers a reorganization: Management moves stem from performance concerns—Helping Fiorina "succeed." *Wall Street*

Journal, Sect. A1.

17. McCartney, S. 1995, January 31. Management: Michael Dell—and his company—grow up. *Wall Street Journal,* Sect. B1.

18. Zachary, G. P. 1989, December 28. Microsoft's Mr. Inside on outside. *Wall Street Journal.*

19. Ibid.

20. Reed, D. 2004, December 21. CEO Bethune prepares for final approach; Continental chief says he's leaving airline "that works." *USA Today,* 1.

21. Reuters News Service. 2004, July 10. Colgate executive promoted, spurring talk about top post. *New York Times,* Sect. C2.

22. Warren, S., and J. Ball. 2005, August 5. A change of leadership for big oil companies: Raymond turns over reins to Tillerson as Exxon hits height of earnings powers. *Wall Street Journal,* Sect. A3.

23. Machalaba, D. 2004, September 29. Norfolk sets plans for '06 succession by naming a no. 2. *Wall Street Journal,* Sect. B3.

24. Executive shuffle at Delta. (2005, July 21). *Atlanta Journal and Constitution,* Sect. A1.

25. Stock, B. 2001, November. Improving the CEO succession process. *Corporate Board Magazine.*

26. Blout, E. 1996. Polaroid: Dreams to reality. In E. Blout (Ed.), *The power of boldness.* Washington, DC: Joseph Henry Press.

27. Roth, S. 2004, July 2. Kauffman Foundation's executive changes continue. *Business Journal* (Kansas City), 3.

28. Hofmeister, S. 2004, July 3. Los Angeles Times, Sect. C3.

29. Kirk, J. 2004, July 15. McDonald's is poised to expand duties of 2 top executives. *Knight Ridder.*

30. Dow Jones Newswire (2005, June 10).

31. *CIO* magazine (2005, May).

2

HOW IS THE CHIEF OPERATING

OFFICER ROLE USED TODAY?

[Lord Uxbridge:] As I am second in command and in case anything
should happen to you, what are your plans?
[Duke of Wellington:] To beat the French.
From the film Waterloo (1970)

As noted, it is our contention that there are various ways in which companies approach designing the leadership team generally, and specifically the content and context of the COO position. Here we offer five descriptions of organizations that illustrate some of the variety we found. At Walt Disney, the loss of Frank Wells and subsequent efforts by Michael Eisner to find a number two and heir are discussed. Then, the oft-hailed leadership succession efforts of IBM and Intel are considered. Next, Microsoft is used to illustrate having a COO to complement the CEO. Finally, Carly Fiorina's experience at Hewlett-Packard describes the challenges that result when a decision is made to go without a COO in a turbulent, competitive business.

WALT DISNEY

In 1994, Disney's president and second in command, Frank Wells, tragically died in a helicopter crash. Wells and Chairman and CEO Michael Eisner had been hired together in 1984 by Disney's board of directors.[1] The two successfully ran Disney with essentially a co-leadership model. Each had great respect for the other's leadership and decision-making abilities. For a number of years, they were an example of how two people could work together successfully to lead a complex, multifaceted organization.

In that same year, Eisner was faced with replacing his studio chief, Jeffrey Katzenberg. Katzenberg left the company when it was obvious he would not immediately be replacing Wells.[2] Instead, Eisner took on the added role of president. Over time it became apparent—especially as the company eyed acquisition of ABC/Capital Cities—that simultaneously serving as chairman, CEO, and president was far too great a task to vest in a single person. In 1995, Eisner courted and eventually hired the renowned agent Michael Ovitz to replace Wells as president of the company. One could argue that Eisner made this decision without a clear understanding of the way to properly structure and then fill the COO role, perhaps because a quick decision was needed (at this time, Eisner remarked to Director Ray Watson, "What I'm doing now looks crazy: no president, no CFO, no treasurer. . . . ") and perhaps because insufficient attention was paid to developing potential internal candidates.[3] Consequently, Eisner hired Ovitz without thoroughly evaluating the need for a president, the responsibilities the president should take on, and the degree to which there was a good fit between the Disney culture, the company's needs, and Ovitz.

Eisner realized relatively quickly that Ovitz was not the answer. The situation deteriorated rapidly. Though he had known Ovitz for twenty-five years, Eisner failed to invest the time to get to know him in the context of Disney, and he neglected to help with his assimilation into the company—an especially critical mistake at a company with so much history, so many competing egos, and such a strong and distinct culture. Two key executives met Ovitz shortly before he joined Disney and made it clear they would never work for him.[4] Eisner admits he did little to smooth the transition or build support for Ovitz. Shortly after Ovitz joined, he discovered he and Eisner were unable to agree on responsibilities; clearly, role design had been neglected.[5] Frustrated, Ovitz reportedly said to Eisner shortly after joining Disney that he had "no real authority to do anything . . . no real investment in anything creative."[6] Ovitz began to derail early, almost before he started, and eventually Eisner would write a memo to the board commenting that the man he once said could succeed him as CEO was "emotionally and mentally not appropriate for the task."[7] Eisner would add, in a letter to Ovitz, "We started having differences right from the beginning which I attributed to some misguided over-enthusiasm."[8] Many questioned Ovitz's fiduciary commitment as well, as he spent large sums on lavish parties and office redesigns.[9] It didn't help that, when grilled on his "duty of care" obligations as director, he stated, "I'm sorry, I don't really understand that."[10]

In the end, these longtime friends split up unceremoniously, with Eisner commenting to the board that Ovitz "has a character problem."[11] This short-lived CEO-COO configuration broke down early and very publicly, though considering the way the situation began it should have been little surprise.

In 2000, Eisner appeared to have made a better choice for the number two slot at Disney: Robert Iger, the former COO of ABC/Capital Cities, which Disney acquired in 1996. After the acquisition, Iger served as chairman of ABC while simultaneously running Disney's international business. He built a reputation for operating success and efficiency through consolidating and standardizing processes and platforms. At various times in his career, he launched creative programming, turned around businesses, executed strategic acquisitions, and worked effectively across all operations of the business, including sports, television, international, and entertainment. He was a one-company man for his entire career. In short, he had credibility, stability, and know-how, characteristics that were very important. In addition, Disney seemed to get other parts of the configuration right: all key executives, including the chief strategist, would report to both Iger and Eisner. Thus, the organizational structure conveyed the appearance that the two were aligned and equally capable.

Though it seemed to have more promise than the Eisner-Ovitz arrangement, the Eisner-Iger configuration still bore some of the hallmarks of a suboptimal CEO-COO partnership. Iger had been the number two at ABC and was expecting to be the chief executive when the Disney acquisition dashed those plans. It seems well known that he sought the top position at Disney as soon as he was named president in 2000.[12] It can be dangerous for the number two to look past the current role to the top job. It is also interesting that the two did not appear publicly to be aligned; it is Eisner who has been the primary target of public scrutiny and shareholder outrage, while Iger has managed to stay off the radar. If the true test of a successful CEO-COO configuration is its performance against the market, or against peers, it might seem that the Eisner-Iger tandem has not been tremendously successful.

As of early 2005 Disney seems to be turning the corner. The Disney board unanimously elected Iger after a thorough external search that yielded some of the most successful, highly accomplished executives across a range of industries. Also, though Iger had his eye on the CEO role for some time, he indicates that he was not looking past his current responsibilities. In 2004 he publicly remarked that the Disney board should consider him as a successor to Eisner "based on one thing and one thing only . . . the performance in the current job I have. I'm concentrating on the job I have in hand."[13]

So, in the end, it appears that Eisner may have done well, both in selecting Iger as a number two and in eventually nominating him as the CEO succession candidate. After all, once Iger was offered the role, board Chairman George Mitchell remarked that he "had the right combination of company knowledge, candor, and experience dealing with others to move this company to another level."[14] Given the complexity of Disney's business operations, the strong personalities involved, and the unique culture that permeates the organization, Eisner and Iger must have been aligned on at least some things. Clearly, they got some—though certainly not all—elements of a successful CEO-COO configuration right.

Time will tell if Iger's tenure as chief executive is successful in terms of value creation and restoration of the iconic company. Though the Eisner-Iger CEO-COO configuration was more successful than its predecessor, it is still the result of an incomplete process. Perhaps Iger will further develop and employ the process as he considers the option to add his own number two.

IBM

In 1993, IBM broke with its tradition and hired outsider Lou Gerstner, a former RJR Nabisco and American Express executive, as chairman and CEO. It was clear from the outset that Gerstner's job would not be easy. He would be leading a high-profile and storied company. IBM was looking ahead, beyond the desktop PC era, and grappling with the client-server "revolution." The Internet age was presenting seemingly enormous but undefined opportunities. On the operating side of the business, the company was beleaguered by financial underperformance; cost management would be a critical issue going forward. Gerstner would have his work cut out for him, and given that the challenges focused on industry-specific issues and included unpopular cost containment decisions, it was likely that his outsider status would make his job even tougher.

Making matters more complicated, the situation inside IBM was difficult.

The company had just seen its annual net losses top $8 billion; exiting CEO Jim Akers was criticized for neglecting to dismantle the company's bureaucracy, reverse its inwardness, and address its culture of entitlement. Though something had to change, an outsider CEO who had grown up in consumer products and financial services was not immediately hailed as the answer to IBM's mounting problems. Even the *Wall Street Journal* called the appointment of Gerstner "audacious."[15] Interestingly, with all of these pressing challenges ahead of him, Gerstner made it a priority shortly after joining IBM to focus on an issue that was not at the top of the list for many people: his own succession plan.

Rather than launch a brand new plan he could put his own stamp on, Gerstner recognized that—given the uncertainty and anxiety characterizing his arrival—some sign of continuity would be critical. He also recognized that IBM possessed a great deal of highly capable talent. Thus he sought to continue upgrading the CEO succession plan initiated by his predecessor. Gerstner quickly concluded that Sam Palmisano, one of Akers's favorites within the company, was indeed the rising talent that Akers thought he was, and he made Palmisano his right-hand man.

By confirming Palmisano's designation as a high-potential executive, Gerstner helped his own cause. The move could be interpreted as a signal to an anxious organization that this outsider CEO was not bent on upheaval and radical change. The move also indicated that Gerstner knew his predecessor had done many things right, including identifying a talented potential successor. It signaled that he was not interested in institutionalizing selection of outsiders for the top job and that he held great respect for the traditions of Big Blue. Finally, by teaming with Palmisano and supercharging his development, Gerstner made it clear that he knew IBM was a place filled with talent capable of leading at all levels—especially at the very top.

Though Gerstner can take a lot of credit for Palmisano's development as a CEO candidate, much of the effort predates Gerstner's arrival. Akers appointed the young man as his executive assistant. Later, he sponsored Palmisano's move to Japan, where—as senior managing director of operations—he was one of only a few IBM executives to lead overseas.[16] During the Akers and Gerstner eras, Palmisano went on to run the high-profile PC division, the server and storage group, the moderately profitable outsourcing subsidiary, and eventually the company's consulting and systems integration business. This last group he restored to profitability within a year and formed what was known as IBM Global Services, a shining star in the IBM portfolio.[17] The development of Sam Palmisano was deliberate, well planned, and effective— and it spanned two very different leadership eras. Initiation of this thoughtful succession plan is a real credit to Akers, and continuing and upgrading the plan is a testament to Gerstner's smart leadership style. His deliberate efforts to acknowledge IBM's past and his willingness to take the time necessary to evaluate the talent of his incumbent executives were both very important.

Although Palmisano was certainly a promising executive, Gerstner took some personal risk in upgrading his succession plan. In 2000, he carved out the president and COO role—the number-two job in the company—and installed Palmisano. To help create room for a bona fide number two, Gerstner moved John Thompson into a vice chairman spot, where he would focus on identifying and developing future opportunities for the company.[18]

A key feature of these changes was that they were driven by strategic and business needs; IBM was becoming ever more customer-oriented and market-sensitive. At the same time, the future of technology in general appeared to be as promising, yet as uncertain, as ever. Overarching these two characteristics was the need for strong leadership and guidance. The best approach for the business was therefore to station Palmisano to help lead operations and Thompson to focus on long-range opportunities while Gerstner provided strategic leadership. When the announcement was made, Gerstner stated, "As we enter the next phase of IBM's transformation, we need a new organizational approach that will strengthen our focus on both day-to-day marketplace results and future growth opportunities."[19]

Of course, Gerstner (and others) recognized the difference between himself and Palmisano. According to one analyst, Palmisano was "much more easygoing than Lou Gerstner. He likes audiences, whether they are his peers or underlings. He likes the atmosphere of give and take. When he enters a room, it doesn't get quiet, whereas when Lou Gerstner enters a room, you know he's there to make a speech."[20] Yet Gerstner was not so ego-driven or insecure to think he had to select a clone as his successor or let Palmisano's development plan lapse in order to dissolve any threat to his authority. At the same time,

Palmisano understood his responsibility as the number two. Though he must have known early on that he was a high flyer and potential successor (the role of executive assistant to the CEO is known to be a key station on the path to the job at IBM), Palmisano took on each role and made the most of it, focusing on the tasks at hand. This is a theme echoed by many: a COO who is more concerned with trying out for the CEO position is likely not putting the company's interests above his or her own.

As Gerstner and Palmisano led together, they did so in a complementary fashion, with Palmisano focusing on day-to-day operations and Gerstner leading strategy and steering the company toward greater customer and market sensitivity. Though different, the two were in basic agreement on many key elements. Palmisano began his career in sales, and Gerstner was very sensitive to orienting IBM to the customer. Stylistically, the two had commonalities as well. According to one analyst, Palmisano was "similar to Gerstner in that they don't believe management should be foilware—wonderful presentations and slides."[21]

In March 2002, Gerstner stepped down as CEO, and Palmisano took over the top job. Palmisano was elected chairman-designate in October of that year and assumed duties as head of the board in January 2003. In the end, the fact that Palmisano was the company's future CEO was a critical realization; according to some, it was one of the few things John Akers and Lou Gerstner had in common, but it was enough to ensure the right leadership was in place at IBM.[22]

INTEL

In March 1998, Craig Barrett was named chief executive officer at Intel. It would seem that the changing of the guard at one of Silicon Valley's most successful technology companies is quite newsworthy. However, the move passed without great fanfare. Instead, the real debate that sprang up centered on who would ultimately succeed the newly promoted Barrett as CEO once he eventually left that role. Though this may seem odd to some, those familiar with Intel understand. The tech stalwart is, after all, one of the most methodical, forward-thinking, and transparent companies of them all when it comes to CEO succession. Intel believes that a CEO transition should occur with mini-

THE CHIEF OPERATING OFFICER ROLE TODAY | 25

mal disruption.[23] The company should not be distracted by anxiety over who will lead next; energy and resources should remain focused on making the business successful now.

Intel's methodical and highly successful CEO succession plan has roots in the company's early days. When Robert Noyce co-founded Intel in 1968, he already had on staff the CEOs for the next thirty years. Recognizing the deep talent pool within his own company, he decided the best answer to the CEO question was likely to be down the hall. Noyce set a precedent of designating internal high-potentials for intensive grooming and smooth transitioning into the top jobs, believing this was a more promising strategy than evaluating unknown, external candidates for a successor role at his unique company. The strategy has proven successful, resulting not only in world-class CEO leadership but also in minimal disruption to firm operations during each transition process. Since Noyce identified his successor more than thirty years ago, the board of directors has made planned CEO succession a top priority, if not the top one. Today, the process is thorough, ongoing, and involved. According to Director David Yoffe, the board discusses executive changes "ten years out to identify gaps"—gaps that are then filled through experience, mentorship, and study. In addition, at the beginning of every calendar year the board evaluates more than twenty Intel executives, assessing the performance of each in his or her current role and also the potential of each to lead as the CEO.[24]

This internal focus enables a thorough review of each potential candidate. The board believes it is better to intensively evaluate an exclusively internal candidate pool than to dilute focus on a broader pool of talent. Another feature of this approach is that it mitigates the risk of one or another director advancing a particular outsider. The seriousness with which the Intel board takes CEO transition is impressive. Yoffe calls CEO selection the "single most important role of the board" at Intel.[25] To ensure success, the board insists on identifying the successor far in advance of any public announcement. This is coupled with the measured transition of responsibilities to the heir apparent, who undergoes a process of title accumulation, taking on the COO title and then that of the president, before officially becoming the CEO. Throughout the transition, the CEO-designate operates as the right hand to the chief executive, gradually taking over top job responsibilities. This enables the successor to learn CEO duties on the job but away from public scrutiny, flying under the radar; the CEO (by title) continues to serve as the public face of the company. Gordon Moore, who succeeded Noyce, in turn handed off CEO duties to Andy Grove in a gradual way; Grove was named president in 1979 but did not become CEO until 1987.[26] Craig Barrett, who succeeded Grove, became a director in 1992, COO in 1993, and president in 1997, all before becoming CEO in 1998.[27] All the while, his responsibilities grew until he ascended into the top role seamlessly. Predictably, Barrett began handing off key responsibilities to Paul Otellini long before it was announced in 2004 that the latter would be the company's next CEO. In the Intel tradition of gradual transitions, this announcement came a full year before Otellini actually took on the CEO title. In advance of that announcement, he led as general manager of the key Architecture Group at Intel and was named director, COO, and president in 2002—an appointment clearly designed to signal he was the heir apparent.[28]

Part of what makes Intel's CEO-groom-for-transition process work so well is the fact that the company's exiting CEOs and incoming heirs apparent respect the process and understand their responsibilities within it. First, CEOs are measured by the job they do in developing a successor. Then, as the transition is made in stages, the CEO-designate understands that he or she will be doing many parts of the job as a test of sorts before earning the title. The successor must also understand that he or she is to actively seek mentorship from the sitting CEO, and accept advice that is given. The CEO-designate must also commit to upgrading skills to those expected at the "C" level. Otellini, for example, began a battery of intensive study sessions through which he augmented his technical knowledge.

Intel's exiting CEOs, however, have perhaps the greatest responsibility for ensuring a successful transition. They must be ready to move on while at the same time mentoring their successor and abdicating the "right" duties. For example, among the responsibilities that Barrett handed off to Otellini were capital projects, which are highly visible endeavors that are critical to Intel's operations and were well within Otellini's capabilities. Unafraid to eschew key activities and fully aware of his successor's capabilities, Barrett made the best choice for the development of the incoming chief.

Though Intel's CEO succession management has been quite successful, some consider the early identification and long transition process risky.

Whereas such a long, methodical process generates little disruptive fanfare, an early announcement may serve to discourage talented executives viewing themselves as candidates for the top job.[29] This has indeed happened at Intel, but the conclusion reached is that postponing the inevitable adds no value. In fact, the company's exclusively internal and straightforward approach most likely fosters respect and allegiance. In addition, Intel's phased approach has another benefit: The measured transition gives the company time to plan not only for the CEO changeover but also for any executive departures that might be precipitated by designation of the heir apparent.

MICROSOFT

In early 2002, Microsoft announced that President and Chief Operating Officer Rick Belluzzo would resign on May 1. The news came as a surprise to many, and as it broke pundits tried to explain the move.[30] There was a sense that Belluzzo's departure was symptomatic of a bigger problem at Microsoft.[31] Specifically, the company was described as being unable (or unwilling) to welcome and assimilate outsiders into top leadership roles.[32] Though it is true that since Bill Gates brought in his first outside top executive twenty-four years ago there have been a number of configurations of seniormost leadership, upon closer inspection the idea that Microsoft rejects outside leadership seems less valid. Nor does it appear that the frequent leadership changes at the very top have been disruptive. To be sure, Microsoft has not successfully executed every incarnation of the one-two model. In fact, if you count the "office of the president" and the sprawling "executive committee" arrangements, the sheer number of configurations Microsoft has tried at the top is striking.

In the early 1980s, Jon Shirley was recruited from Tandy to succeed James Towne, who had served for one year as Microsoft's first president. The *Wall Street Journal* labeled Shirley a "classic Mr. Inside" who would afford a "calm, self-effacing balance to Mr. Gates."[33] Shirley was brought in for specific reasons: to mentor the young Gates as his company grew in scale and scope and became ever more visible; to lead the company through the launch of the Windows operating platform; to take the company through an IPO; and to oversee the physical move to Redmond, Washington, where the Microsoft campus would be located.[34] Role design was equally specific, with challenges that were meaningful and attractive to a successful operations executive such

as Shirley. In fact, Gates had already signaled his intention to oversee and engage more with the development side of the business when, in 1982, he added
to his chairman title that of executive vice president in charge of all development. There was a real need for a seasoned executive with specific operations
capabilities. At the same time, Gates was not divorcing himself from the business; if anything, he was becoming more involved.

The Gates-Shirley configuration lasted nearly seven years, through several
key milestones in the company's history. Microsoft shares rose 1,000 percent
from early 1986, when first sold publicly, to June 1990, when Shirley left his
post as president and COO. (By contrast, the Dow grew approximately 100
percent during that same period.[35]) Shirley's success as the number two would
prove difficult to replicate. Michael Hallman, Shirley's replacement, struggled
as second-in-command. The media clearly viewed his selection as being intended to bring some balance to Bill Gates. *BusinessWeek* introduced him
as "Bill Gates' New Mr. Nice Guy."[36] The motivation for creating a COO to
lead a specific strategic objective was also reflected in media reports; the *Wall
Street Journal* noted that Hallman was to push OS/2 as an industry standard.[37]
Though the *Journal* viewed him as a "sober manager" who could lend some
maturity to Microsoft's young management, within twenty-four months he
resigned his role as president and COO, as well as his seat on the board.[38] In a
move that has become fairly typical following a COO departure—and an indicator that the position was ill-conceived—Hallman's duties were split among
three executives who formed the office of the president—what *InfoWorld*
termed the "troika" of Ballmer, Mike Maples, and Frank Gaudette.[39]

In some respects, it is no surprise that the Gates-Hallman configuration was
unsuccessful. The search for Shirley's replacement lasted only four months, a
fraction of the time required to find a COO who can work in the unique culture of Microsoft alongside its hard-charging founder. Also, assimilating outsiders was not a Microsoft strong suit. In 1992, one executive described Microsoft's assimilation process by explaining: "The training we do is on-the-job.
Throw them in, and good luck."[40] Hallman, whose career was spent at IBM
and Boeing, grew up in a navy-suit culture of rigid process and bureaucracy.
When Gates let Hallman go, he said: "I didn't see him as a match for what the
job had grown to. I expect a lot of new thinking."[41] Though rapid change and
role evolution are *de rigueur* in the fast-paced world of software, it seems there

was little time spent up front identifying personality conflicts, cultural differences, role design, and assimilation expectations—key factors about which Gates and Hallman should have been savvy.

However, it seemed Microsoft was determined not to make the same mistake twice—or at least not twice in a row. The company operated with the three-executive office of the president for the next two and a half years, until business strategy dictated the need for a dedicated COO who could rein in the significant operational issues that were creeping up inside the fast-growing company. This patience and market-facing thoughtfulness set the stage for another successful senior-level configuration.

In late 1994, Bob Herbold joined Microsoft as executive vice president and COO, responsible for worldwide operations. His specific functional responsibilities included finance, manufacturing, distribution, logistics, information technology, human resources, corporate services, real estate and development, and Microsoft Press.[42] Most important, Herbold was charged with bringing operational discipline to the company.[43] Like Shirley, Herbold's responsibilities were specific and meaningful. But although they were broader than those of any other Microsoft executive at that time, Herbold did not join explicitly as the number two. Instead, he joined the office of the president, whose membership included longtime Gates confidant Steve Ballmer, as well as a handful of other executives.

This placement would prove to be critical to Herbold's success at Microsoft. It communicated that he was welcome as an insider and trusted—not only by Gates but by the other top executives as well. Just as important, Herbold's place in the organization signaled that he was not brought in to create a new layer of management between Gates and the other operating executives; rather, his position in the company gave the appearance that he was there solely to improve the lives of the operating executives. After all, he would be an outsider—from the rigid culture of P&G, no less—brought in to drive process and systems improvements across the entire enterprise, which had been flourishing under a freewheeling culture. He would need the strong support of Gates's inner circle to be effective. He would need to operate from authority bestowed on him by more than just Gates. He would need the ratification of the longtime leaders of the business.

To Herbold's credit, he recognized that assimilation was his responsibility as well. When he arrived at Microsoft, he was "shocked" by the lack of process and systems coordination.[44] He also realized any initiative that would dampen the company's culture of nimbleness, responsiveness, and creativity would fail.[45] Still, he had a job to do. Herbold understood he had to deliver operational improvements in a way that went beyond preserving the company's cultural asset, to enhance it.[46]

Owing in part to this mind-set, Herbold was a tremendous success at Microsoft, despite the enormous challenge of driving process improvements into a loose and permissive culture. He joined the company as a COO with much to do and never had designs on the CEO role. In fact, when he left Microsoft, after renewing his contract twice, he explained that he had no interest in becoming a CEO.[47]

Though Herbold was a great success by many measures (stock price grew 1,200 percent while the Dow rose 200 percent between fourth quarter 1994 and first quarter 2000), the company realized in 1999 that he would not renew his contract forever.[48] Microsoft then set about to identify Herbold's replacement. In September 1999, the company hired Rick Belluzzo, an accomplished executive trained at Hewlett-Packard—a company whose culture was as process-oriented and operationally savvy as Procter & Gamble's. Belluzzo was brought in first to lead the high-profile Consumer Group and eventually to drive coordination and efficiency into the relationship between development and the field group.[49] This relationship was critical for successful product launch and delivery. However, there were warning signs that might have gone unheeded, which indicated Belluzzo would not enjoy a long tenure, as had his predecessor.

Although Herbold never seemed terribly interested in becoming CEO, Belluzzo was considered in the running for the top job at HP and left shortly after it became apparent that he would not get the job. He joined Silicon Graphics as that company's chief executive before moving to Microsoft. When he left Microsoft, Belluzzo remarked that in his next role he really wanted to run a company.[50] It seems Belluzzo was an executive who was at his best as the chief executive. He was initially placed in charge of Microsoft's powerful consumer group, but functioning as one of a handful of general managers feels very different to someone who considers himself (and in fact has been) a public company CEO.

When Belluzzo joined Microsoft, Herbold was preparing to exit, but before he did Ballmer was moved into the CEO role. Belluzzo would eventually take on the COO title, but fifteen months after doing so, he exited the company as part of a reorganization, a consequence of which was that all business heads reported directly to Ballmer. Since 2002, Microsoft has operated under the Gates-Ballmer model. This marks the first time the leadership structure has been this simple since Shirley was with the company. However, only two years earlier the company had Gates, Ballmer, Herbold, Belluzzo, and the executive committee vying for influence at the top.

Although the change to a simpler design would seem to be quite dramatic, the Gates-Ballmer model is likely to be successful. The two have known each other since they were teenagers, rooming down the hall from one another at Harvard. Ballmer understands Gates's personality, and in fact he mimics his boss's passion, albeit in a more expressive style. Ballmer spent more than twenty years on critical parts of the Microsoft business before joining Gates at the top. He knows the culture and the history quite well and has been validated as a result. He has also worked closely with Gates and other top executives at Microsoft for many of those twenty years, which means he should be able to quickly develop a productive pattern of work relationships.

For a company such as Microsoft, where passion for products and a belief that what you are doing will have tremendous impact on how people live, Ballmer's traits are invaluable. The recent decision to reactivate the COO role, thereby adding a third member (COO Kevin Turner) to the leadership team, suggests Gates and Ballmer realize that even more help at the top will be necessary as the company moves forward.

HEWLETT-PACKARD

In February 2005, Carly Fiorina announced her resignation as chairman and CEO of the $80 billion Hewlett-Packard Company. She joined in 1999 from Lucent Technologies, where she led a $20 billion service provider business. Though having earned a reputation as an outstanding partnership builder and a sales and marketing superstar, at HP Fiorina became best known for advocating and then executing the enormous, but disappointing, acquisition of Compaq—a deal that most would argue led to her ouster.

It is often said that hitting the numbers allows one to ignore small problems; it may be that not hitting the numbers brings additional scrutiny. As HP continued to underdeliver on the returns expected from the Compaq merger, the board decided it was time to get the CEO some help; they began to press harder on the COO issue. Unfortunately, though there were a number of challenges Fiorina could handle as CEO of HP, sharing control of the company was not one of them.

Leading Hewlett-Packard is not like leading most companies. It has always been very visible, a mainstay of Silicon Valley folklore and an icon of both entrepreneurial inventiveness and corporate strength. The company was beloved by many for its product development and ingenuity. Now, with Fiorina at the helm, it was the only Dow component with a female chair/CEO. This level of visibility often makes challenges even more difficult, and the challenges facing Fiorina were many and complex. Dell had formed an alliance with Lexmark in a first step to target HP's lucrative printer business. Shortly after Fiorina joined HP, the tech sector suffered an unprecedented downturn that affected not just HP but also the company's partners, on whom HP was particularly reliant. In addition, the board of directors at HP was rumored to be pretty difficult at times as well. One analyst referred to HP as "the Vietnam of corporate governance."[51] Thus, Hewlett-Packard was a challenging place to be chief executive.

Still, Fiorina seemed adept at dealing with these challenges. Rather, it was the merger with Compaq that was the hallmark of Fiorina's tenure. Before the tech recession ended, Fiorina aggressively pursued the largest tech-sector acquisition ever with its pursuit of Compaq. This was a decision not embraced by everyone. Many analysts opposed the deal, and a Hewlett family heir led a tough and public proxy fight.[52] One reason for the opposition's concern was the fact that a merger—especially a large one—requires intense operational know-how to capture synergy and eliminate redundancy without negatively affecting customer service. This would be especially tough in a complex business such as HP, where the company relied so heavily on third-party partnerships. Having been brought up in sales and marketing, Fiorina did not appear to have the deep experience in operations that is so valuable in a situation of this kind. Though Compaq chief Michael Capellas stayed on as president, it was rumored that he would jump ship once the deal was signed; Fiorina made no attempt to bring in operations talent at the seniormost level. Instead, she pushed ahead.[53] The stage was set for a make-or-break situation that was shaping up to be nothing short of legacy-defining.

Yet, given the challenges, the visibility, and the high stakes, Fiorina refused to address the COO issue. Capellas did indeed leave the company after six months, and Fiorina refused to replace him. In fact, she consolidated power by having those executives who were reporting to Capellas report directly to her. Her continued resistance to the board's desire for a strong COO was identified by observers as one of the fundamental avoidable mistakes of Fiorina's tenure at HP.[54]

As we have described, it takes a lot of work to correctly recruit and integrate a COO. A CEO often must work more, not less—certainly at first and sometimes throughout the life of the CEO-COO partnership—to foster success. In HP's case, there was clearly a business need for a strong, capable number two. This was the largest tech merger in history, undertaken by a highly visible company, before the sector had learned all the lessons of an unprecedented downturn; it was being led against some public dissent by a chief executive who did not seem to have the operational depth required to make a large merger or acquisition work. In summary, the strategic decision to acquire Compaq, the resulting need to closely lead day-to-day postmerger activities, and the opportunity to add to top management strong operational skills to complement the CEO's capability in sales and marketing all argue for creation of a COO role. This was not the conclusion Fiorina reached.

As the Compaq merger delivered results that continued to lag behind expectations, the board was beginning to wonder if the naysayers were right after all. They wanted Fiorina to bring in a strong COO to boost the chances of improved performance. She refused. Though this decision strained her relationship with some of the directors, she likely realized the difficulties and time requirements associated with effectively adding a number two. She also likely realized that attracting a top-quality COO is extremely difficult when the individual does not see an impending opportunity to assume the number one job—a job she had no intention of vacating in the foreseeable future. Perhaps she believed she should not share blame if the merger ended up underdelivering. Still, in the end Fiorina believed a one-two punch in this situation could not succeed. With the benefit of hindsight, perhaps she would have chosen differently.

SUMMARY

The five cases reported in this chapter were selected to help convey the variety in approaches that companies take in structuring themselves at the top of the organizational hierarchy. The Disney case describes two important issues: the difficulty in finding a number two who fits well with the number one and the complicated interpersonal issues that arise through the effort to set up the number two as heir. At IBM, the way a new chief executive was able to retain and then continue to develop a talented heir apparent, ultimately turning it into a model succession story, was reported. The efforts to make leadership succession as much of a nonevent as possible was described using Intel, a company that receives ongoing kudos for its ability to change leaders without, apparently, missing a beat. Microsoft's case is interesting for two reasons. First, over time Bill Gates has tried several COOs, some of whom have brought what pundits consider to be an important balance of skills to the top of the company. Second, Microsoft has been flexible about how it structures itself at the top, moving through various leadership configurations. In fact, as this book goes to press Microsoft has just announced that it is restructuring again to better meet the demands of the company's environment. Now three presidents, Robbie Bach, Kevin Johnson, and Jeff Raikes, will report to Chief Executive Ballmer.[55] Finally, the experience of Carly Fiorina at Hewlett-Packard illustrates the difficulties that can emerge when one individual tries to manage both large-scale strategic issues, such as a merger, and the day-to-day challenges that a large and complex company faces.

In all, the variety in these cases should reinforce our contention that the COO role is a complex one. Knowing when to create the role and how to structure it and understanding the nature of the capabilities an incumbent needs to successfully enact the role all merit further attention.

NOTES

1. Taylor, J. *Storming the magic kingdom.* New York: Knopf, 1987.
2. McCarthy, M. 2004, March 3. Disney showdown is today. *USA Today,* 4.
3. Masters, K. 2004, August 16. Deposed—The strange hiring and firing of Michael Ovitz. *Slate* [Washington Post Newsweek Interactive], 16.
4. Gentile, G. 2004, October 1. Shareholder lawsuit over Ovitz hiring, and firing, airs Disney's dirty laundry. AP Wire.
5. Ibid.
6. Text of Eisner letter to Ovitz. (27 February 2004). *Hollywood Reporter.*
7. Gentile (2004).

8. Eisner letter to Ovitz (2004).

9. Gentile (2004).

10. Masters (2004).

11. McCarthy, M. 2004, November 18. Eisner calls Ovitz actions "despicable." *USA Today*, 4B.

12. Holson, L. 2005, March 14. Disney replaces CEO Eisner a year early. *New York Times.*

13. Iger—Says he would love to become Disney's chief. (2005, August 6). ShowbizData. com 6.

14. Holson (2005).

15. Rozek, V. 2002, March 4. As I see it: Sam I am. *Four Hundred Newsletter* (ITJungle.com).

16. Ohlson, K. 2001, December 24. IBM's CEO-in-waiting. *Network World.*

17. Ibid.

18. Kanellos, M. 2000, July 25. IBM taps new president, vice-chairman. Cnet News.com.

19. Ibid.

20. Ohlson (2001).

21. Ibid.

22. Ante, S. E., and Sager, I. 2002, February 11. IBM's new boss: Sam Palmisano has a tough act to follow. Here is what to expect. *BusinessWeek.*

23. Zachary, G. P. 2004, July. How Intel grooms its leaders. *Business 2.0*, 43–45.

24. Ibid.

25. Ibid.

26. www.intel.com.

27. Ibid.

28. Moltzen, C. F. 2004, November 15. Intel's Otellini to succeed Barrett as CEO next year. *CRN.*

29. Zachary (2004).

30. Wilcox, J. 2002, April 9. At Microsoft, three's a crowd. Cnet News.com.

31. Cook, J. 2002, April 4. Microsoft President and COO Beluzzo [sic] resigns. *Seattle Post-Intelligencer.*

32. Ibid.

33. Zachary, G. P. 1989, December 28. Microsoft's Mr. Inside on outside. *Wall Street Journal.*

34. The History of Computing Project: www.thocp.net/companies/microsoft/microsoft_company.htm.

35. www.msn.com.

36. Meet Bill Gates' new Mr. Nice Guy. 1990, May 21. *BusinessWeek*, 151.

37. Faludi, S. C. 1990, March 20. Microsoft names Hallman president, succeeding Shirley. *Wall Street Journal*, Sect. B10.

38. Zachary, G. P. 1992, February 4. Microsoft says Hallman to quit as president. *Wall Street Journal*, Sect. B1.

39. Picarille, L. 1992. Gates ousts Hallman, puts troika in his place. *InfoWorld*, *14*(6), 6.

40. Rebello, K. 1992, February 24. Microsoft: Bill Gates' baby is on top of the world. Can it stay there? *BusinessWeek*, 60–66.

41. Ibid.

42. Herbold, R. 2002. Adult supervision: Herbold's old-world order for Microsoft. Excerpted from Inside Microsoft: Balancing creativity and discipline, *Harvard Business Review*, *80*(1).

43. Ibid.

44. Ibid.

45. Ibid.

46. Herbold, R. J. 2002. Inside Microsoft: Balancing creativity and discipline. *Harvard Business Review, 80*(1), 72–79.

47. Neff, W. W. 2002, Summer. Innovation and discipline: An interview with Bob Herbold. *Chief Executive,* 12–16.

48. http://moneycentral.msn.com/home.asp.

49. Wilcox (2002, April 9). At Microsoft, three's a crowd. Cnet News.com.

50. Ibid.

51. Dawson, K. 2002, November 12. Capellas jumps ship to helm Titanic? *Media Unspun.*

52. Fried, I. 2001, November 6. Hewlett family opposes Compaq deal. Cnet News.com.

53. Burrows, P. 2005, March 7. Commentary: Ousting Carly was just the start. *Business-Week Online.*

54. Lavelle, L. 2005, February 28. Three simple rules Carly ignored. *BusinessWeek.*

55. Guth, R. A. 2005, September 21. Microsoft to restructure business. *Wall Street Journal.*

A CONVERSATION WITH ED ZANDER

CHAIRMAN AND CEO, MOTOROLA, FORMERLY COO, SUN MICROSYSTEMS

Edward J. Zander is chairman of the board and chief executive officer of Motorola. He entered his position with more than twenty-five years of experience in the technology industry. Prior to joining Motorola, Zander was a managing director of Silver Lake Partners, a leading private equity fund focused on investment in the technology industry. Before that, he served as president and COO of Sun Microsystems. During his tenure, Sun rose to $18 billion in revenues, becoming the number one company in the server market and the preeminent supplier of network infrastructure. Earlier, Zander served as president of Sun's software group. Prior to joining Sun in 1987, he held senior management positions at Apollo Computer and Data General.

AUTHORS: Think back to your days as the COO at Sun Microsystems, and share with us what it takes to be a great leader as second in command.

ZANDER: The number two position is a pretty difficult job because you are sitting right between line operations and the CEO. I think the most important thing for a COO is to understand the job. Too many COOs try to be CEOs or don't fully understand the role of the COO. The first thing that I did at Sun was to understand what Scott McNealy was going to do and what I was going to do. My job was not to be him.

I think what a COO does is just what the job says—operations—that is, execution of the plan. To me, it was very simple. I had to make the quarters, get the products out the door, hire the right people, and organize according to the business plan. That is not to say you don't play an important role in strategy, acquisitions, architecture of the company, and other outside activities, but by and large that is secondary to your role.

The primary role is to complement the CEO by making the results, helping set the plan, and executing. Of the three things that I practice here at Motorola—vision, focus, and execution—the CEO largely is chartered with the vision of where the company is going, establishing the goals and objectives, and implementing the architecture of the company.

AUTHORS: **What about the way you organized the company? Who were your direct reports, and who were Scott's?**

ZANDER: At Sun, this was very clear, but it was a problem at Motorola. When I joined Motorola there was a box on the organizational chart called Office of the Chairman, which comprised the chairman, CEO, and president. I don't have any problem with a structure such as that; however, it was odd for me having been the COO at Sun.

At Motorola, the first day I came in, the head of HR and the head of finance were not sure who they worked for because of the two-person office structure. Clearly, each company is different. As the COO at Sun, I had the businesses reporting to me—manufacturing, sales, engineering, and products. The CFO, HR, CIO, legal, and corporate development and IT architecture functions reported to Scott. Building the products, manufacturing the products, selling the products, supporting the products and services/field services was in my world. We met almost every day to talk about things. I had an open-door policy where Scott could come to my staff or my strategy meetings and was not threatened. I invited Scott to participate in anything that I was doing. He knew he was welcome to any of my meetings, and he never felt as though he was excluded from the strategy or business decisions I was making.

There is another important difference between being CEO and COO that also became clear to me when I joined Motorola. As the CEO, you need to focus more on external audiences, and for my first few months at Motorola I spent a lot of my time talking to customers and employees. Throughout my career, I have always believed in placing the customer at the forefront, but as CEO it is even more critical.

Motorola has tremendous strengths, but they will be wasted without understanding what the values to our customers are. The need to understand customers is especially true for technology companies because we are all working to deliver the "next big thing." Companies don't just develop technology for technology's sake; in listening to customers and markets, companies in turn can develop meaningful technologies and turn them into products that make customers winners and keep markets evolving. As CEO, I ask myself and challenge my team to think about the customers, and I see my interaction and understanding of our customers as one of my most important tasks.

AUTHORS: One of the things that can go wrong when reporting is unclear is that people try to get a "back door" to the CEO and try to get a different decision. How do you prevent that?

ZANDER: First of all, you have to be comfortable with yourself. If you are insecure as a COO, forget it; don't be one, because it is going to turn into a very difficult job. The same is true for the CEO. The deal that I had at Sun was that any one of my direct reports could go to Scott, talk about things, Scott could call them up, and it was never a closed door. One thing that Scott did very well was to never undermine me—he never undermined me in a meeting, and he always backed all my decisions. He would hear people out but then send them to me. If Scott heard something that he didn't like, he would come in and talk to me about it. We worked really well together in that regard. There was a solid wall between us and the rest of the company. That said, I wanted Scott involved because he was a really smart guy on strategy and on vision and I wanted engineering VPs or sales VPs to hear what he had to say.

AUTHORS: Why are there so often COOs in technology companies?

ZANDER: That's a good question. I think the reason is because a lot of the CEOs were founder/entrepreneurs that weren't schooled in years and years of management. In technology start-ups, the smart CEOs realize that running a $10 billion or a $40 billion company is taxing.

I believe there are a lot of articles being written about COOs, saying they are out and not needed anymore. During the first year at Motorola I wanted to stay close to the action and close to the businesses. I was very aware of and realistic about the challenges that Motorola faced both internally and externally. I asked a lot of questions and spent a lot of time listening. I remember feeling invigorated by the challenge of improving Motorola's operating and financial performance.

In tech especially, where it is all about product, strategy, disruptiveness, and customer needs, getting close to the action is critical. I felt with a COO that I was one level removed from sitting down and talking product strategy with the businesses. So the usefulness of the COO role—at least to the CEO—depends on the state of the company. What shape is it in? If this thing is humming along, I may want to spend most of my time meeting with customers and employees—the things that are driving the strategic direction of the company. If you think you have more stuff to go do—and I do here, around supply chain, taking costs down, getting product strategy in place, getting the right people in the right jobs—then the COO could be a problem.

AUTHORS: Is there a natural life span for the number two?

ZANDER: I think there is. I used to say five years, but now I believe it's three or four years. The reason is very simple. After three or four years, my feeling is that you start to think more and more about the CEO decisions. I started to think to myself, *I would buy this company. I would change the compensation.* I knew the strategy direction I wanted to take. That's how I knew it was time to move on.

AUTHORS: You are now the CEO and have been for a while. What didn't you learn as the number two that was the biggest surprise becoming the number one?

ZANDER: There is no substitute for experience. I've been around for a long time and know that it never seems as good as it is and it's never as bad as it seems. We've made great progress at Motorola, but we've still got a lot of work left to do.

Another thing I've learned is that as a COO you can't fully understand the pressure of decision making; it stops with the CEO. No matter how many decisions I made at Sun, and I made a lot every day, there are decisions that only the CEO makes. The day I arrived at Motorola, January 5, 2004, I started making decisions and there was nobody above me. You have to live with those decisions, and that is probably the toughest thing in moving to a CEO position as a former COO.

A CONVERSATION WITH CAROL BARTZ

CHAIRMAN, CEO, AND PRESIDENT, AUTODESK

At the time of our interview, Carol Bartz served as chairman of the board, president, and CEO of Autodesk, the world's leading supplier of design software. Under her leadership, the company has diversified its product line and grown revenues from $285 million to $1.234 billion in FY2005. Before joining Autodesk, Bartz held a variety of positions at Sun Microsystems, including vice president of worldwide field operations and being an executive officer of the company. Previous to her time at Sun, she held product line and sales management positions at Digital Equipment Corporation and 3M. She also serves on the board of directors of Cisco Systems, Network Appliance, and the Foundation for the National Medals of Science and Technology. Among her many distinctions, she was named in 2004 and 2005 by Forbes magazine as one of the world's "100 Most Powerful Women" and was also on the BusinessWeek "Women in Technology" list (http://usa.autodesk.com/adsk/servlet/item?siteID=123112&id=348263).

AUTHORS: What first comes to mind when you consider the keys to success for someone in a COO position?

BARTZ: I personally think that the best way to ensure success of the COO is for the CEO to select someone you either are working with now or have worked closely with in the past. That way, each understands the working style of the other. Going into the relationship, there is a shared understanding of where there is going to be overlap, deficiencies, etc. As an example, John Thompson at Symantec brought in John Schwartz as COO. Though I personally wouldn't have arranged for a COO quite as quickly as he did, John (Thompson) had worked with him before and probably thought—and with hindsight rightly so—"With two of us in here, there will be four ears and four eyes working on things. That way, we can get this done a lot faster. Because I know you, I trust that you are not going to be spending your time climbing up my back to try to get my position." As a result, he felt safe enough to bring a COO on board.

One other thing I have never quite figured out is why a CEO would create a COO position before having had some time themselves with their own hands on the operation. I think a CEO has to get familiar enough with the business so they don't feel the COO has blocked them from the business. I think if I had come into Autodesk as the new CEO and immediately appointed a COO, it would have been as if I'd said, "I am really not going to get that close to this business and I don't care deeply about our operations." Instead, it makes more sense to me—in terms of timing—for the CEO to learn the business backwards and forwards while grooming someone to come on as COO. For me, once I had established myself, and once my COO candidate (Carl Bass) was ready, it was then time to create the position.

AUTHORS: When you created the role, was your vision to free up your time to focus more on Autodesk's future or to provide opportunities for Carl to develop as a potential successor—or both?

BARTZ: Both. It's important for potential successors to be in a position to spend time with the board so they develop relationships and become comfortable with one another. That said, does it give me more time? Yes.

AUTHORS: Sometimes people who formerly reported directly to the CEO resist creation of a COO position. How have you worked through that tension?

BARTZ: I did that in half-steps. Three years ago, our sales organization was separate from the product divisions. The two leaders—the worldwide sales guy and the head of the products—were trying to run a joint staff, trying to work out the sales engineering issues, and so on. It wasn't working. So I solved this by appointing Carl to run the design solutions group. In effect, I put 80 percent of the revenues of the company under Carl three years ago, beginning the restructuring that led to changes in reporting relationships. But I tell you, just to go cold turkey and make the announcement of a COO, there is way too much to work out for that to be a successful approach.

AUTHORS: How do you manage disagreements that come up between you and Carl? How important is it to keep them behind closed doors?

BARTZ: Well actually, we don't have to do that. We can differ in public and one of us knows to compromise. I actually think that is healthy. I'll go rant and rave about something. For example, tomorrow we have a joint CEO/COO staff meeting. I can tell you that at some point in the meeting I'll be saying something and maybe Carl will say, "Well, we ought to think about this and that," and I'll say, "Fine." Or perhaps I'll say, "No, I insist." The latter only happens maybe 5 percent of the time because normally we either agree or he talks me down.

AUTHORS: You have served as a director at Cisco at two parts of their life cycle. From that experience, what are your observations regarding the structure John Chambers has implemented? There currently are five senior VPs, but no COO or obvious heir apparent. Is there anything to learn here that might apply to other firms, or do you think Cisco is just a unique situation?

BARTZ: I think when you have when you have a youngish CEO who has a lot of runway left, you have to be very careful about making declarations or allowing assumptions about who is heir apparent. The candidates will just start bumping against the top and each other; as a result, they don't know what to do with themselves and you get a very political organization. You either have to accept that some unannounced, potential heirs are going to go off and become CEOs at other companies or you have to figure out a way to still keep them in the box. Of course some won't want to be a CEO, some are likely so close to John that they are just fine with him still running the company. And, by the way, that is a hard time for the board because you are suppose to be doing your succession planning even though you know logically you don't have your CEO retiring for a long time.

AUTHORS: A situation similar to the one you just described is FedEx. Fred Smith has probably had three or four COOs who went on to be CEOs elsewhere and he has just continued to run the company. From the board's perspective, he has built bench strength along the way, just in case.

BARTZ: As a board member, I would see that as totally acceptable. The CEO has to say, "I am going to groom people." A consequence of grooming good people is that some—perhaps many—of them are going to go off and be successful somewhere else. That is certainly the problem you have in Silicon Valley; they always want to go off.

AUTHORS: A bit earlier you mentioned the importance of the COO having a role with the board. What is the best way to structure that?

BARTZ: At Autodesk we only have one insider on the board, and that is me. I have had a rule for my tenure that my staff must attend half the board meetings a year. I was giving the board access to the VPs before that was a common thing to do. Once I had given Carl this even bigger position three years ago, he began coming to every meeting. As COO, he presents at every meeting. Some time ago, I began sending Carl to dinners alone with the board so that they could get to know him better. He was a little uncomfortable at first, because his opinion is independent; he is not—nor do I want him to be—a Carol clone. His words are going to come out differently than mine, his opinions can be different than mine, and they can ask him whatever they want. Now, at this board meeting coming in March, we will go to dinner together with them. He was alone for the last two.

AUTHORS: One of the consistent themes across our interviews is the importance for the CEO to be comfortable giving this sort of autonomy to the COO.

BARTZ: You have to. If you are not, if you have any little vestige of whether your job is safe or paranoia, believe me you are going to kill a number two. You are just going to kill him. Those situations, where the CEO and COO either let a fissure get in between them because they make decisions that are against each other, or the CEO just can't give up the control or doesn't really want a number two, are disastrous for all involved. Sometimes, the CEO realizes intellectually that they want a COO but they can't operationally have one—they can't develop enough trust.

AUTHORS: What about the life span of a COO? Is there one?

BARTZ: There probably is. I think sometimes it depends upon the kind of things they get to do. I would think a COO who isn't being challenged wouldn't want to hang around very long. For instance, I have Carl on this challenge now of figuring out how we want to do development abroad. It is a big strategic initiative within the company. I know from my experience that Carl gets into trouble if he is not busy. In fact, I just put the CIO under him.

AUTHORS: Would you describe your skill set and Carl's as complementary, overlapping, or identical?

BARTZ: I would say overlapping. He is more technical than I am. I am not nontechnical, he is just more—he has never managed sales, and that part of the operation is new to him. Part of what I had to do for the board to support the COO role was to promise that I would really help him with sales. Carl and I both like numbers and like to dig, so there is some overlap, but we are clearly not identical or redundant in terms of skills.

AUTHORS: Would you comment on what you have observed about how founders deal with the COO role and the heir apparent? You had a chance to work with Scott McNealy at Sun Microsystems, and you have obviously viewed other founders such as Marc Andreessen (Netscape). Are there any observations you have made about how that might affect a number two role?

BARTZ: I think anybody taking a number two role from a founder is nuts. You need to have an age gap like there was at Netscape between Jim Barksdale and Marc. Look at Eric Schmidt and the Google founders. The only reason Eric gets along with them is he lets them do what they want. He is not running that company. He is just the guy with the tie. If you take over after a founder, that is a whole different story. At Dell Computer, Mort Topfer had a successful run with Michael, but here again was a big age difference; Mort was fifty-six and Michael was twenty-eight—and everyone knew Mort wasn't going to be CEO. In that case, you have someone who basically states, "I am here to help. I really will run the company for you, but I am not going to try to kick you out."

AUTHORS: Another very high-profile example involves Ray Lane and Larry Ellison at Oracle.

BARTZ: Ray was never going to be the CEO at Oracle. Even board members used to say that "Larry will leave Oracle when they take him out in a pine box." The problem is that I am not sure Ray necessarily believed that. Larry at some point had to take Ray out and did, because Ray was getting too much credit. As the number two, you can't take credit. Mort did not try to take credit.

A CONVERSATION WITH JOHN BROCK

FORMERLY CEO OF INBEV AND COO OF CADBURY SCHWEPPES

John Brock recently stepped down as CEO of InBev, a global brewing company. InBev has a portfolio of more than two hundred brands, including Stella Artois, Brahma, and Beck's, its three global flagship brands. It employs some seventy-seven thousand people and runs operations in thirty-two countries across the Americas, Europe, and Asia Pacific. In 2004, InBev realized a net turnover of more than €8.57 billion. Brock joined Interbrew in February 2003, bringing to the company almost twenty-five years of experience in the global beverage industry. He started his professional career at Procter & Gamble and then joined Cadbury Schweppes in 1983. There, he held a number of senior positions in various geographies, was appointed to the Cadbury Schweppes board in 1986, and became COO in 2000 (www.inbev.com).

AUTHORS: Thinking back to when you were in the number two position at Cadbury, can you give us some sense of the key competencies associated with being successful in that role and how they might differ from those you must exhibit now as CEO at InBev?

BROCK: I think, frankly, the role of the COO and the role of the CEO in terms of the key competencies one needs are not dramatically different. First and foremost, chief operating officers have to be very skilled at wheeling and dealing with people—leading people, motivating, providing incentives, and getting them focused on a common agenda and a common set of objectives, all supporting a business vision. Most COO roles are a bit more executional in focus, and you have to be good at that. But in the end, it is all about leadership and people, and frankly, you have to have those for both the CEO and COO roles.

AUTHORS: Please talk a bit about the relationship between the COO and the CEO. How does that relationship need to be set up so that it works?

BROCK: I think it depends upon the reason why the COO role was created. The company, its CEO and its board ought to think carefully through why they want to have a COO. If you have some clear reasons to have a COO, then I think it can work, and friction between the CEO and COO is not inevitable. Let me give you a couple of examples. I think if it is made clear that the COO is the leading candidate to become CEO and this plan is recognized and supported by the board, then my sense is that you have a more effective COO position. Some firms seem to create the role to just see how it is going to work out. I see those two as very different situations; the latter will be dismal for the COO.

Another example: If the company is very much an M&A-driven machine and that activity is really the focus of the CEO and he wants a COO to run the business while he and his CFO are off making deals, I think that would work. Also, if you have a situation where the CEO has too many direct reports—which is often the driving force for creating the COO—and there is a view that "Gee, let's simplify that and not have as many direct reports," that can work. Finally, one other situation I have come across, not in my own experience but have seen work, is when you have a more statesmanlike figure who is appointed to COO. Everybody knows he is not going to become the next CEO.

When I joined InBev, there was a COO in place and one of my first orders of business was to eliminate that role. Four months after I joined, it was clear to me that I wanted to be closer to the business. I didn't want one person running the entire business. I convinced the current COO to take a different position, and in the end that worked fine. I would not have been happy, nor would he, under the scenario where he remained as COO.

AUTHORS: We talked to Ed Zander, who used to be the number two at Sun Microsystems and is now the CEO of Motorola. He had a number two when he came into Motorola and did the same thing you did as one of his first moves. He did not want a number two because he wanted to be close to the business for the first few years.

BROCK: That is exactly what I did. And it is a painful situation. I have twelve direct reports. I have five zone presidents and seven chief staff officers—finance, legal, commercial, technical, etc. Twelve direct reports are too many. But on the other hand, there are none of those positions that I want to combine, and similarly, I want to be close to the five zones.

AUTHORS: Zander said he might have a number two in three years or four years, but right now he needs to run the business.

BROCK: That is exactly my view. And part of that for me was the change in direction of InBev. We had gone, prior to my time, from being the seventeenth-largest brewer in the world to number three in volume over a ten-year period. So the company had been a very effective M&A machine. My predecessor and the board had decided that it made sense to have a COO so he, the CEO, could focus on acquisitions. When I joined the company, my view as well as the board's view was, "Let's really run the business; let's focus on organic growth and efficiency improvements and ultimately, shareholder return." That was a large part of thinking behind removing the COO position.

AUTHORS: If the COO is passed up for a vacant CEO position, is it time to leave?

BROCK: That depends. If you are someone who has a clear agenda to become a CEO, yes, it is an inevitable move that if you create a CEO and it is not the guy in the COO position, then you have just cut his legs off. In most cases, unless you have gone into it clearly with the idea that the COO is in fact not going to be the CEO because of a variety of age or other kinds of issues, then I think inevitably you have created a problem.

AUTHORS: When you think about your transition from being a number two and then becoming the number one, what were the biggest surprises?

BROCK: Two things come immediately to mind. First, the substantial level of really critical interpersonal interaction with the board of directors that comes about by being CEO—the need to orchestrate, coordinate, and deal with the intricacies of that. For me, that is a real, key part of my job. Even though we are publicly traded, we have three Belgium families and three Brazilian families who own over 50 percent of the shares. It is important for me to maintain an effective relationship with them and keep them involved and informed (utilizing our nonexecutive chairman as appropriate from a governance point of view). That is a huge difference from anything I dealt with as COO.

CEO   The second key difference is being so immersed in the relationship between vision, strategy, and values. Knowing where you want to go and how you want to get there, and how that fits with the values of the company is critically important. As COO, the "How do you get there?" was a big part of the job. The focus was executing business strategies and turning in really good, solid business results. Not unexpectedly, the CEO requires more strategic thinking, a clear vision, and dealing with a board. As I said at the outset, I think the people component is the one piece I would say is *not* that different. My sense is that any position of substantial responsibility in today's corporation is heavily people-intensive. At the end of the day, that is what it is. It is figuring out who the right people are, as Jim Collins says. It is figuring who ought to be on the bus that is more important than, frankly, figuring out where you want to steer the bus. If you have the right people, then remarkably they will help you figure out where you want to go. If you have the wrong people, you have no chance.

AUTHORS: When you were the number two, and there was a layer between the typical direct reports to the CEO, how did you manage that?

BROCK: Most of the time it worked out fine. I think it really comes down to how capable and flexible the people skills are of the people involved. Managing that relationship depends upon the personality and style and people skills of the CEO, the COO, and then the people that report into the COO. The team I had assembled at Cadbury Schweppes was outstanding. I had been there for twenty years and was chief operating officer the last three and a half. Before that, I had run the beverage business. If you took a look at the people I had reporting to me across the world, they were all hand-picked—two that were hired from outside, but mostly people I had selected from inside the company. So I had a team of first-rate people who were totally confident in their own skills. I would say it goes back to whether or not you have a team of people reporting to you as chief operating officer who are totally comfortable and confident and not too egocentric. If that is the case, then generally you'll not have any reporting-related problems that can't be overcome pretty easily.

AUTHORS: We have heard from others that some of those former direct reports to the CEO try to find a back door on decision making, or possibly create tension between the two.

BROCK: That is absolutely the case. If I had had a situation where more of those guys were not people I had personally groomed and brought along, I think that would have been more of a challenge—particularly if you had someone who had been hired from outside as a COO. Hiring a COO from the outside is something I would be very reluctant to ever do. That would be asking for a problem. By the time the new COO learns the situation and the people, it may be too late in that some bad habits have likely been established.

AUTHORS: Where we have seen successful COOs come in, they often come in as U.S. Operations, president of U.S., president of something, and then they have migrated into the number two role.

BROCK: I totally agree. Or if you hire somebody as a COO, again with a very clear understanding that within eighteen to twenty-four months the plan is for them to be CEO and all of the visible signs and signals that emanate from the board and the current CEO support that, then I think that could work fine.

AUTHORS: What does a good CEO look like if you are a number two?

BROCK: It gets back to the point of why the COO role was created. I think it is hard to say without that. If the COO role is created because you are the CEO-elect, then a good CEO is basically someone with whom you as COO share power. When the COO visits a market, for example, if the people there knew it is not only the COO but in a sense the CEO who is physically there and speaking and saying things, it makes it easier for the COO. As COO, you want a relationship with the CEO so that everybody knows that when one or the other speaks, it doesn't matter which one you are hearing. What you are not going to want as COO is a case where the CEO pays a visit to our operations and comes back and writes a two-page memo listing all the things that were wrong with the business. That shows you don't have agreement between the CEO and the COO on what are the respective roles, and that is counterproductive.

AUTHORS: Will you ever have a COO at Inbev?

BROCK: I am not against the role. I think there is a real possibility here at Inbev that we may recreate the role. On the assumption that I am around here for several more years, I would like to work with the board to decide who my successor is and, to the degree we can be clear and appoint him as COO, I think that would make a lot of sense.

A CONVERSATION WITH KENNETH W. FREEMAN

MANAGING DIRECTOR, KOHLBERG KRAVIS ROBERTS & CO.
FOUNDING AND FORMER CHAIRMAN AND CEO, QUEST DIAGNOSTICS

Ken Freeman recently joined Kohlberg Kravis Roberts & Co., a leading private equity firm, as a managing director. Previously, he was the chairman and chief executive officer of Quest Diagnostics, the nation's leading provider of diagnostic testing information and services. Freeman has been credited with executing a major turnaround and subsequent growth strategy at Quest Diagnostics that put the company in a leadership position in its industry. During his nine-year tenure, the company's market capitalization increased from $350 million (at the time the company was spun out from Corning) to more than $9 billion (http://www.kkr.com/news/press_releases/2005/05-03-05.html).

AUTHORS: When you began as CEO at Corning Clinical Laboratories, you did not have a COO in place. Why was that?

FREEMAN: I arrived on the scene in May of 1995 at what was then known as Corning Clinical Labs, a wholly owned subsidiary of Corning Incorporated. The business was broken. My job was to turn the business around. One and a half years later, Corning spun us off to its shareholders. It turned out to be a much more significant turnaround than anyone had anticipated. I decided it was very important *not* to have a COO during my early days at the company, from the beginning of May of 1995 until Surya Mohapatra arrived in early 1999 as senior VP and COO. [*Note:* Mohapatra succeeded Freeman as chairman and CEO in December 2004.—Authors] My belief was that in a turnaround situation, when everything is broken—relationships with the government from a compliance standpoint, relationships with customers, relationships with employees—to have more than one cook at the top giving direction can confuse people to no end. I was the president and the CEO and the chairman in the early days of the company, until we had turned the company around sufficiently so that all constituents could see that the company was making good progress and was on the road toward success as opposed to failure.

As we went through those years, I evaluated the internal talent. I did not see people on the inside that could ultimately be the number two or the number one in the company in a time frame that was consistent with my view of the world. I didn't want to be in the job more than eight to ten years because I believe that CEOs become value destructors rather than value creators if they stay in the job too long. Individual leaders can only drive so much change in an organization. Someone else may be better suited to drive the company to the next level. I began looking outside the company in mid-1998, to bring in a person who would be my number two and could someday potentially be the CEO. But by no means was I going to hire someone and guarantee that they would be the CEO five years later. You are always evaluating your choices—other internal candidates, benchmarking against outside candidates as well.

AUTHORS: What were you looking for in that potential heir?

FREEMAN: I was looking for a person who had a different collection of skills from mine. At the top, what you don't need is a bunch of people who are identical. Although you must insist on a strong value system grounded in integrity, you need people with different points of view and experiences who can collectively drive progress in the company.

Surya and I "interviewed" each other seven times before he joined the company. We met face to face on most of those occasions and talked by phone on others—all over the course of six months. We had our first encounter during the summer, and he joined us on February 1, 1999. During that time, I was also working to transform our business, negotiating with SmithKline Beecham to acquire their testing business. Jan Leschley was their CEO at the time. In the summer of 1998—the same time I started to talk to Surya—I was negotiating with Jan to buy his lab business, which at the time was the biggest and most rapidly growing competitor in industry. So here we were, going from surviving and turning a company around to taking undisputed industry leadership. At the same time, I was looking to find a potential COO.

In my own mind, I thought that in a company that was going from $1.5 billion in revenues to $3.2 billion if we closed the deal, from roughly twelve thousand to roughly twenty-five thousand people, it would be helpful to have somebody around that had strong health care experience. Especially given that I had grown up in the glass business! I was a financial guy, did turnarounds left and right, but hadn't really been a health care guy until Corning sent me to the lab business.

So over six months, Surya and I had our seven discussions, and we worked through the process of gaining trust with each other. One of the last discussions we had before we both agreed he should come to Quest Diagnostics was about the definition of our roles and responsibilities. It was clear to me from our dialogue that he aspired to become CEO of a significant health care company. For him to leave Picker International—where he was very successful and highly regarded—he would have to see that potential. It was also important to me that he understand that I wasn't looking to hire someone who in one year was going to take my place. I was looking to bring in a person who would become a trusted partner and teammate as we took the company from being one of several large competitors in an industry where there are five thousand small competitors to becoming the undisputed industry leader.

We went through a diagnostic where we said, "Let's talk about the roles, who is going to do what," and we came to a general agreement on what our roles and responsibilities would be. That was vital and helped avoid what can inevitably be pain and agony for any company: lack of clarity at the top.

We announced Surya's arrival as president and COO to the world on February 1. We announced the acquisition of SmithKline's lab business about two or three weeks later. I told him on the day he accepted the position that "the company you are joining is now going to be a little bit more than twice its previous size!" Surya was dumbfounded and even more excited, as you would expect.

So what does this all suggest? It is not necessary to have a COO in place at all times. There are moments, such as turnaround situations, when it can be very damaging for a company to appear to have more than one ultimate leader at the top. It can slow things down, and the internal conflict between two people is not easy to hide if it exists. But there are moments in any company's history where it is entirely appropriate to have separate CEO and COO roles. In February 1999, four years into my tenure at Quest Diagnostics, I felt it was appropriate to establish the COO role for two reasons: one, I was looking someone who could potentially be my successor down the road, who brought complementary skills including science and technology in their background. And I was about to lead a company that overnight was more than doubling in size and complexity. We didn't have the internal talent pool to run it effectively, and I wanted a teammate at the top helping me drive the company forward.

AUTHORS: What about the need for direct reports to create a back door around the COO to the CEO? Was that an issue you and Surya had to deal with?

FREEMAN: In the early days, that was certainly an issue. Employees and managers are accustomed to having direct access to you, the CEO. Until you "prove" they report to the COO, they are still going to try to reach to you for decisions and everyday support. Hence there is a critical need not only for clarity of role definition between the CEO and COO but also for clear communication of those roles and responsibilities by both parties. It goes beyond just stating the different roles, because in the end we are all reasonably poor listeners. All the talk has to be reinforced with behavior. For example, when a former direct report who now reports to the COO comes to you and says, "I know we haven't talked about this, but I just want to get your advice." The job of the CEO has to be to push back and say, "Look, I need you to work through the COO. It is not that I don't support or respect you, it is just that for driving our company forward you need to take your leadership to Surya and he has my complete support."

This is easier to say than it is to execute, because everybody, even the crustiest CEO who is the most arrogant guy in the world—and they are out there—loves to be loved. We all love to be loved. We want people to come say we need your help and want your assistance. And when you have come through a turnaround, you are used to giving all the answers because the company needs one person on point to do it. Surya and I defined our roles, made it crystal clear throughout the organization, and kept each other honest all the way through.

AUTHORS: Given that Surya came from outside and you did not have a work history together, how did you build the trust in the relationship?

FREEMAN: Building trust takes time. Given that we were new together in 1999, we didn't have a lot to build on other than a common belief in the importance of integrity, teamwork, and accountability in leadership. What we ended up doing was deliberately carving out a substantial amount of time to have one-on-one conversations. Sunday at 4:00 P.M. became the time for us to have lengthy discussions about what was going on in the company, what was going on in our lives, for me to have opportunities to provide coaching for Surya, and for us to learn from each other. These weren't face-to-face discussions. We would see each other at the office too, of course, but there we would be scurrying around working on the integration of the companies, driving the company's performance and making things go. We had each other's undivided attention via telephone starting at 4:00, virtually every single Sunday for five years. That built a huge amount of trust between us. We could call the question on any issue at all. If Surya said, "I think people are coming to you on these issues" I could say, "They are, Surya, and here is what I am telling them, I am telling them to come to you." Or if either of us saw something that needed to be shared, we did so. We built incredible trust between each other based on open sharing with each other. In the back of my mind, I thought Surya could potentially at some point become the CEO of the company—I wasn't looking to stay in the job for twenty years. I view my success as my successor's success. I think he saw that behavioral attitude in me, so it gave him reason to say, "I will trust him; maybe I do have a shot at becoming CEO here."

AUTHORS: In addition to your time on the phone, what about physical proximity? Was that important to you?

FREEMAN: Close physical proximity is vital. Surya and I were in adjoining offices. We used a shared administrative assistant's model where each of us had our own assistant but our backup was the other person's assistant. We worked as a team, not only he and I but our assistants as well. We forged a team environment so there wasn't a lot of hide and seek, there weren't any hidden agendas. We had a very open book with each other. Our collective goal was to create value for customers, employees, and shareholders.

AUTHORS: We have heard from COOs that there sometimes is a moment where they really understood they had complete trust of the CEO, and that it was a key moment. Ed Zander, when he was the number two at Sun, clearly remembered the first time he was sent by Scott McNealy to fix a significant problem. He said, "Wow, he is putting me out there and this is a great opportunity." Is there a moment where that happened for Surya?

FREEMAN: From my perspective, there were a number of different moments. I treated his role as COO in part as a developmental assignment for him. I would constantly send new and different challenges his way. I found it exciting to see him grow. I am sure he felt great about it too. This included everything from negotiations with our largest customers to presenting at investor conferences. When I handed him the ball in the early days he would say, "Are you sure you want me to do this?" I would say "This is all part of your development. It is going to be a great experience for you." As we moved further down the road, he got more comfortable with that and flourished in it.

Another area that gets kind of interesting, particularly when the COO is going to be potentially the CEO, is how you engage the board in the process. In our case, in the early days Surya would go to the board meetings with other members of management and was reluctant to speak out in a way that was different than what I—as CEO—was saying. I worked to create opportunities for board members to have dialogues with Surya when I was not in the room. In board meetings, I would sometimes leave when he started presenting so there would be no possibility that after his presentation a board member would turn to me and ask me what I thought. I made little adjustments that in retrospect sounded so silly but were so real, like changing the seating in the board room so Surya was interspersed with the board members. I put Surya at the table, and sent him out into the field to meet privately with each director one-on-one. These kinds of activities gave him more confidence, and gave the board the opportunity to see him in action. At the end of the day the board makes the decision about who is going to be the CEO. It built his confidence, and the board's confidence in him.

AUTHORS: Is there a natural life span for the COO role?

FREEMAN: I think there is, although I wouldn't have said so a few years ago. If the COO wants to become a CEO, there is a time limit. That said, there is also a place for permanent number twos in a lot of companies.

AUTHORS: Just look at Colgate; Reuben Mark had the same number two for twenty-plus years.

FREEMAN: It can work, but it takes a special number two who says, "Being COO is my job and I know I don't want to be the guy in front of the analysts every quarter or whatever it is in terms of the CEO's roles and responsibilities," *and* believes that he or she is better behind the scenes than out in front. It also takes an incredible partnering relationship between the CEO and the COO. I think that is more the exception than the rule.

As to the COO life span: I believe for a person aspiring to become the CEO who enters a company from the outside, as opposed to having grown up inside the company, three to five years, maybe six should be the limit. If they don't get the job by then, they should probably leave. In Surya's case, he had been COO for five years when he got the call to become CEO. He came to Quest Diagnostics from another company where he had the potential to become the CEO, and he came with the goal to become CEO here. You don't want a COO sitting there, itching like crazy for six to twelve months, saying "When is this guy going to get out of here? I have proven that I am the guy; is the board reluctant to make me CEO, or is Ken reluctant to leave? Something is not right here. Maybe I should just go somewhere else." There is no shortage of opportunities for COOs to become CEOs at other places if they perform well. The key is to be able to assess your COO and other potential successors to make sure they are not really a permanent number two who thinks they should be number one.

You don't really know that you have a winning CEO until he or she actually has the title and is in the job. I remember saying to Surya on the day before he was appointed CEO, "You know, I have been working for five years to get you ready, and you have been working for five years to get yourself ready. There is no question you are going to be successful, but believe it or not when you become the CEO, the view will change. It is uncanny. You are as prepared as anybody can be, Surya, but the view changes when you are in the number one job. The buck now really does rest with you. There is nobody to go check in with, nobody to go say, 'What do you think?' It is all in your lap."

AUTHORS: I am sure you have had discussions with him since he has become CEO. How has his transition been?

FREEMAN: Very, very smooth. The company continues to perform exceptionally well. The company has transformed from being a grower primarily through acquisition to being a grower primarily through organic growth in addition to selective acquisitions. All the financial metrics are very positive, and within the organization the management team has done a great job of forgetting the founder, if you will—me—and latching onto the new guy as the number one guy, in Surya. A part of that means the former CEO has to get out of the way, not show up, not be in the headquarters building, not be visiting the laboratories, not be in the chairman role very long, if at all. I was chairman from May until December 2004—during Surya's first six months as CEO—the last step in the transition. It was very clear to everyone that I was there to run the board, *not* the company. We took Surya through a deliberate development process. The final phase was for me to serve as a confidential sounding board for him as the newly anointed CEO, without any ramifications.

AUTHORS: What advice would you offer for CEOs thinking about creating a number two position?

FREEMAN: Don't do it just because you think you want some time off. Do it with a business purpose. Perhaps you need somebody who brings complementary skills as you take your company through its evolution. Perhaps you have been CEO for a long time (in my definition, that means eight to ten years), are getting serious about identifying a successor, and want to put an existing high-potential from the inside or somebody from outside in the COO role to move the process along. Have concrete reasons—real, tangible, business, and company welfare reasons to have a COO. If you are not ready to share the power, don't do it. That said, if the business situation dictates a need, you better get going, and find the very best COO business partner you can!

A CONVERSATION WITH MIKE LAWRIE

FORMER CEO, SIEBEL SYSTEMS

Mike Lawrie succeeded founder Tom Siebel as CEO of Siebel Systems, a position he ended up holding for just less than one year. Before joining Siebel Systems, he spent more than twenty-five years in global operations with IBM. During that time, he held numerous sales, marketing, development, and financial management positions. In 1997, he was named IBM's general manager for personal software products and later headed the Network Computing Software Division at a global level. In 1998, Lawrie became general manager for IBM in Europe, the Middle East, and Africa (EMEA), where he led a team of more than ninety thousand employees with responsibility for sales distribution and services operations in 124 countries. His last position at IBM was senior vice president and group executive, sales and distribution, where he led the company's global operations.

AUTHORS: Can you describe for us through your own experience the key competencies required to be successful as a top operations executive?

LAWRIE: One, you have to be able to check your ego at the front desk. You have to get real comfortable with someone else getting a lot of the limelight as a result of work that you have done. That is one key point. Second point, the number two has to provide a good balance with the number one guy. In other words, if the CEO is a great strategist then you better be, as the number two, a real good executor. If the CEO is a great executor, then you better be a pretty good strategist. I have found that if the number one and number two complement one another well and then they divide the responsibilities up based upon their competencies, then it can work reasonably well. Where it doesn't work real well is if they both are pretty good at the same thing and they both are focused on the same thing. That is what leads to conflict and confusion in the organization.

Selflessness, a good balance with the number one person—those are two of the more fundamental things. Then there are three other things that I think are critical. First, they have to be obviously very competent; they have to know the business—they have to get it. They have to know the industry; they have to know the competitors, and so on. Second, they have to be able to lead collaboratively, not hierarchically. The more collaborative they are as a number two, the better they can get the organization to function. And third, I think the number two has to be performance- and results-oriented.

AUTHORS: What have you observed about CEO-COO relationships and what makes them work?

LAWRIE: If the CEO is a good coach and is really looking to grow executive talent, and has a reasonable succession plan in place, then I think that can work very well. Where there is often a problem is where the CEO views the COO as the on-deck hitter. If he feels like the board is just waiting for the third strike and the new guy comes in, that can lead to a great deal of tension in the relationship. I think the board has a very important role here too. The board needs to make it clear that the CEO is the leader and that there is no ambiguity in the organization as to who is running the organization.

The number two role is often used for succession planning and development. You have to set that up for success, both from the board level and from the incumbent CEO. The board has to understand the purpose of the COO role. Let's take IBM, where I have some experience. Lou Gerstner put a COO in, Sam Palmisano, for two reasons: One, IBM wasn't performing very well from an execution standpoint and Sam had good execution capability; and the second thing was, we needed a good succession plan to Gerstner. The board was behind that, but the board made it clear to Sam that the future CEO job was not guaranteed. When I was at IBM, I sort of was the de facto number two, but the board saw it differently. I had to lead much more collaboratively across the organization to get things done because I was not viewed as the successor to Sam. And furthermore, Sam and I were good at the same thing; we are both execution-oriented guys.

AUTHORS: In this whole mix, the CEO's ego and how comfortable they are in their own skin is an important piece of this as well.

LAWRIE: Oh, there is no question that if the CEO is insecure, unsure of what needs to be done, it can be a very volatile situation. If, on the other hand, when the CEO is very secure, is confident, has a good game plan in place, then the probability of taking on more of a coaching role with the number two is much higher.

AUTHORS: What about decision making between the two? Who should make which sorts of decisions?

LAWRIE: Certainly, the roles and responsibilities have to be clear in order for the organization to execute. In my mind, there are really five or six levers that a CEO has to have his hands on and be ready to pull. One is the strategy; is the strategy right? Two, you have to create a solid financial model for the company. Third, managing the scale of operations through acquisitions and divestitures requires the CEO's hands. Fourth, is the identification and development of the leadership team in the CEO's court? This is important—when I see problems between number one and number two, it is often the next level down, the real senior leadership team, who are making the problems. In short, when they are the CEO's people or are the COO's person, and not team players, trouble is inevitable. Then culture: Who sets the tone for the culture in the organization? Is it the CEO or is it the COO? My belief is those five or six levers I just gave you need to be the purview of the CEO. The CEO may go to his senior management team, may go to his COO to help make those decisions or solicit input into the decision-making process, but fundamentally the accountability needs to rest with the CEO. If it doesn't rest with the CEO—in other words, if it is mixed—then all these other things gets screwed up.

AUTHORS: You get the ambiguity. . . .

LAWRIE: You get the ambiguity. And there is nothing worse in an organization in my opinion than when there is great ambiguity over who is doing what, between the number one and number two.

AUTHORS: What are the gaps that you experienced in moving from the number two job to the number one job? How well does the number two experience set you up for the CEO job?

LAWRIE: I wouldn't use my experience at IBM as the best example, because my "number two" designation was more of an informal role than a formal role. That said, yes, I do think it sets you up well. At the same time, there is a different scope associated with being the CEO. You are fundamentally responsible for the company. That rests on your shoulders. The investors, shareholders, press, analyst, customers, and employees—they are all looking to you. There is nothing that can fully prepare you for taking that full emotional burden on your shoulders. It is an entirely different feeling. You own it. The number two position can prepare you mechanically; it can prepare you to understand how things work. I worked at IBM; I understood how the board worked; I understood how we worked with Wall Street; I understood how we worked with our shareholders. I did it, some of it, but if you didn't have the ultimate responsibility for the outcome of it, it is a different emotional zip code when you own it as opposed to participate. It can teach you the mechanics, it can give you intellectual side, but it can't give you the emotional side.

AUTHORS: After having been in the CEO role, what was the biggest surprise to you?

LAWRIE: The biggest surprise . . . that is a good question. There are so many unique things about what I have done here at Siebel. I have a board that wasn't completely understanding of the environment this company was really in. I'm following a founder who was somewhat in denial as to where the company really was. So I have a unique set of challenges, which I not only have to change the mind-set of the employees, but I have to change the mind-set of the founder and the board.

AUTHORS: What about advice for people moving from a number-two-type role into a CEO role. Do you have advice for new CEOs?

LAWRIE: If you are going from number two in one company to number one in the same company, you are a continuation of the some of the same things. If you go from number two to number one in another company, then I think it is very important that you step back and you decide which levers need to be pulled to get the organization moving in the right direction—and I go back to those five or six levers that I mentioned earlier. You can't go in blind or naïve, you have to do your due diligence, understand the financial model, the business model, and so on. You see, I came into this thing and I knew I had to do something with the financial model. So I hired McKinsey to come in and do that. That work is done; we are executing it. I knew I had to do something with the strategy, so I took the team off and we came up with basically a new strategy. I knew I had to come up with a new leadership team. I worked to attract a new leadership team. I knew that I had to go focus on our whole acquisition and de-acquisition strategy because it was haphazard. Because there wasn't a business strategy; the acquisition and deacquisition strategy didn't match the business strategy. So I think as a new CEO, you have to go through and look at things from that context and decide, "Gee, what really needs to change here?" The other advice is I think you have to make that decision relatively quickly because after you are there six months or so, if you haven't really begun to question and stake out a new direction, it gets increasingly hard to do.

AUTHORS: **Can you identify any general guidelines as to when a firm would want to create a COO position?**

LAWRIE: You would certainly want to think about it if you are trying to test somebody to get them prepared for the number one job; that much is clear. Number two, if you are trying to really fill a deficiency that the CEO has. For example, a very visionary CEO who can't execute, that is probably a pretty good environment for a COO. I would say that it is either to fill a blaring organizational or executional issue or it is to get someone prepared to go do the number one. It becomes part of the succession planning process. For example, I have no intentions of having a number two because I am going to build a much more horizontal, collaborative team, and if I put a number two in I would completely destroy that. Fundamentally, you have to decide where do you want to manage contention in the organization. Does the CEO want to manage that contention, or do you want that managed at the COO level?

3

THE JOB OF THE NUMBER TWO

I would rather be first in a small village in Gaul than second in command in Rome.
Julius Caesar

Just as organizations display varying motivations in creating a COO role, how the role is designed and how it is enacted by incumbents vary too. There is no agreed-on description of what the job contains, what it entails, or what it is called. As one executive shared with us, "You can define the job any way you feel like, depending upon the individuals and what you are trying to accomplish." Robert Herbold, who served as COO at Microsoft, told us he doesn't "think there is a single thing as a role called 'chief operating officer.'" Instead, he commented that "there is a constellation of responsibilities that can be put together to create a job that easily carries that title." This variation within the position makes it a difficult one to study; it can be hard to understand if you are making a proper comparison between one COO and another. The purpose of this chapter is first to describe the variations we encountered through our interviews, so that we develop a sense of the boundaries within which the role operates. Then we consider the nature of the challenges we would expect incumbents to face in the role. As you will see, some of these challenges are typical of those you would expect between any pair of supervisors and subordinates. Others are largely unique to the CEO-COO dyad, in part because of the nature of the roles and in part because of the prototypical personalities of the individuals likely to inhabit these roles.

THE CONTENT OF THE COO JOB

In an effort to build a foundation for their look at the COO role, Cannella and Hambrick relied on Mintzberg's framework of managerial roles.[1] Briefly,

Mintzberg developed a typology that included ten roles argued to be inclusive of the range of behaviors required of a manager.[2] Cannella and Hambrick sorted those ten roles as, they felt, involving (1) activities internal to the operation of the firm (leader, disseminator, disturbance handler), (2) activities external to the firm (liaison, spokesperson, negotiator), and (3) internal and external components (figurehead, monitor, entrepreneur, and resource allocator). They report that their work supports the commonsense notion that the COO role is primarily created to address the internal operations of the firm, freeing the CEO to concentrate on tasks that involve representing the firm to external constituents. Our interviews largely support this description of the division of duties.

From our research, three clear models for the content of the COO position were quickly identifiable. The most common structure was what could be considered literal implementation of the title: the COO as the "inside" person, responsible for virtually all elements of the day-to-day operations of the firm. This set of duties creates for the CEO the opportunity to focus energy on both constituencies external to the firm and efforts around developing and communicating the vision for the firm's future. In some—but not all—of these cases, the CEO also becomes a coach and mentor for the next generation of leadership talent. Such was the case at Pepsi after CEO Roger Enrico created the number two role for now-CEO Steve Reinemund. The second structure—not so commonly used, but widely cited—is the two-in-a-box model, where essentially two executives function together as one to co-lead the company. This is certainly a difficult model to implement because of the complexity of, and deep trust required in, the relationship between the two leaders. Two examples of this configuration are Michael Dell and Kevin Rollins at Dell and Bill Gates and Steven Ballmer at Microsoft. Through his tenure as CEO, Gates has had multiple COOs before moving to the two-in-a-box configuration with longtime trusted executive Ballmer. A number of COO positions did not fall neatly into either of these descriptions. The variation among the positions was considerable; what they had in common was a structure that resulted from consideration of the talents of the incumbent, the CEO, and the situation faced by the firm. This last type, what we label "situational," is the most prevalent and (because of the heterogeneity reflected in the position) the most difficult to speak about definitively. As an example, Bob Herbold told us, in describing his time as COO at Microsoft, "The chemistry between the individuals has to be very good. . . . Those shared expectations as to 'what are you responsible for' and 'what am I responsible for' are so fundamental to making the leadership work."

This sentiment was echoed by Joe Leonard, the CEO of AirTran, who told us, "I really very strongly believe that the structure has to be fluid and fit with the current personalities and pressing needs of the organization."

The question that naturally arises from this distinction is whether and how the critical success factors for COOs might be differently arrayed in each instance. For example, when the COO role is designed to oversee operations, the best candidate is clearly someone who has demonstrated that he or she can lead and manage operational detail and deliver results day in and day out. Such an individual understands the operational levers of the business, is results-oriented, and is nearly obsessed with timely production of product, cost control, hiring the right people, leading the team quarter to quarter, and ensuring execution of strategy. To be effective, this COO needs to (1) establish credibility with the operational people at all levels, (2) be a strong communicator, (3) be capable of managing several things at one time, and (4) be able to make sound operational decisions. Typically, successful operational COOs have done many of the jobs of those who now report to them. As a result, subordinates cannot easily pull the wool over their eyes. Finally, these individuals must be able to manage upward to develop productive relationships with the CEO and board. At the end of the day, the best test of the effectiveness of a truly operational COO is his or her ability to consistently execute on all minutiae of the business. Clearly, what is being described is someone with both industry and company knowledge. This job requirement is hard to find in an external hire and as such suggests that one factor to consider in predicting the success of a COO should be whether he or she came to the position from inside or outside the company.

Alternatively, if the intent is to design a two-in-a-box model, the degree to which the COO can rapidly establish a trusting relationship with the CEO becomes the most critical element of the job. Here too, filling the job is rarely accomplished through appointment of an outsider. In our research, the only instance we could identify where such a step worked was the appointment of Mort Topfer at Dell. Rather, such an outcome is generally the result of an evolutionary process through which individuals develop a bond over a long period of time. This is arguably the case at Microsoft, where Gates and Ballmer have a long shared history, and now at Dell Inc. with Dell and Rollins. In a two-in-a-box situation, the precise strengths of the best COO candidate are now defined primarily by what the CEO presents as weaknesses (whether it be leadership experience, operational expertise, or something else) and secondarily by the demands faced by the firm. The trick here is finding the right balance between a situation where the CEO and COO do not have enough in common to set the foundation for a trusting relationship and the situation where the skill set is so similar that the COO adds little value to the tandem. As Charles Wilson told us, "You can't afford to have your number one and number two basically both doing the same job." An example of this done well is described by Mort Topfer (in Chapter Five):

> I think that if people are too similar in skills set, that could create a problem. As it turned out at Dell, Michael focused on the technology of the company; he focused on the interfaces with the Street; he focused on the customer relationships because he did really well at that. He really had no interest in running the company on a day-to-day basis and getting very much involved in the operations and things like that. When I joined the company it was a $2.8 billion company and had never done a three-year plan and never did an annual plan, and it wasn't because they didn't want to do it.

Finally, the key competencies required in what we label here as the situational COO are precisely that—situational. In the first case, where the focus is on operations, the competencies are defined primarily by internal operational demands. In the two-in-a-box model, the competencies are defined primarily in relation to those of the CEO. In the final case, the competencies are often determined by the situation, involving factors internal and external to the firm. In this instance, theoretically insiders and outsiders may each be successful in the COO role. Even still, there is agreement that the skill set is complex and difficult to quantify. Bruce Stein, who served for many years as COO at Mattel, told us:

> In some ways, the COO has to be the consummate plate spinner. Those plates include the day-to-day operations, achieving basic profit-and-revenue goals,

dealing with personnel and operational details, etc. Equally important in the mix are some larger plates, which make a strategic difference to the company. If all you have is someone who is comfortable with the process of managing operations, then perhaps you don't need the COO position.

CHALLENGES FACED BY COOS IN THEIR JOB

Developing a Trusting Relationship with the CEO

Throughout our interviews, the finding is unequivocal: The most critical predictor our executives offered to explain the effectiveness of a COO is development of a trusting relationship with the CEO. Trust is characterized by an expectation held by each party that the other will not, through words, actions, or decisions, behave in a way that takes personal advantage of the relationship. Trust develops over time; in trusting another we assume a risk by making ourselves vulnerable. Research on trust has found that the key drivers making one trustworthy are perception of integrity, competence, consistency, loyalty, and openness.[3] In our interviews, we heard a number of examples of how critical this trust is and how it develops. For example, Craig Weatherup commented that he and Roger Enrico built their relationship and trust when they were working together in Asia earlier in their careers. The times were incredibly tough, but together they survived. Bruce Chizen and Shantanu Narayen built trust while Narayen occupied a number of positions inside Adobe under Chizen's leadership. Later, Narayen was named president/COO. Many of the people we interviewed used the imagery of "having one another's back." This relates to the concern COOs often described involving the efforts of other top managers—many of whom previously had a direct line reporting relationship to the CEO—to circumvent the COO. As described by Wendell Weeks, COO at Corning:

> There are those in organizations who are always seeking to drive wedges if they can. It is not good for them; it is not good for anybody. It is something in the human psyche that seems to like the drama or at least to watch the drama unfold. As a result, the relationship between the CEO and COO has to be really tight one. If they are not able to establish trust or there are inconsistencies in behaviors and actions this can quickly become a derailment factor for the number two and sometimes for the number one as well.

More broadly, the COO candidate must carefully consider what it will be like to work so closely with the CEO. Given the complexity and nuance that characterize the partnership, it is important to evaluate the likely nature of the relationship on a number of dimensions, not just trust. The candidate, we think, is well advised to stay away from a COO position if he or she cannot conclude that the CEO is clearly excellent, as well as committed to helping the COO be successful with regard to goals for his or her tenure.

Building Effective Communication at the Top

The number one and number two have to communicate with each other, formally and informally, so as to be completely in step with one another. Informal communication can be accomplished or at least facilitated by design. For example, locating CEO and COO offices next to each other increases the likelihood of interaction. Dell and Rollins take this to the extreme with a shared office space. One CEO we interviewed stated that a key mistake he made was not having the president/COO's office next to his. As a second example of informal communication, CEOs and COOs talked about habitually bcc'ing one another on e-mails as one way to keep each other on the same page. Through efforts like this, a shared understanding of the fundamental issues was allowed to continually evolve. Then, when they had the chance for face-to-face meetings, time could be spent directly on the issues at hand, rather than on bringing one another up to speed. Formal communications happened most often through planned weekly meetings and teleconferences to ensure strategic alignment. Not surprisingly, most of the executives we spoke to said they communicate through formal and informal channels. Where frequent, effective communication patterns cannot be achieved, it presents a significant risk of derailment for the number two. Over time, the COO will likely move out of alignment with the CEO, and friction will often follow. This in turn can lead to confusion among organizational members. Bill Nuti, now the CEO at NCR, summed it all up well, noting:

> The relationship between the CEO and COO is an interesting one. The first thing the COO needs to do is establish credibility—with the CEO, but also with the top management group. Communication is a key to establishing this credibility. If you communicate well with the CEO, if you understand the vision and the goals of

your CEO very clearly, if you have worked out with your CEO the internal plan to achieve those goals, then you both are in sync. Even more importantly, if you have a CEO who understands that he or she needs to allow you to do your job, you are even better off. Over time, you continue to meet regularly and communicate very openly with your CEO.

In establishing credibility with other members of top management, you must know that there are going to be some who have long histories and close relationships with the CEO. You cannot ignore that. And frankly, you cannot try to get in the way of that. You have to expose the team transparently to the CEO as much and as often as they would like to be exposed. At the same time, you must make sure they understand their role in achieving the goals and objectives that match your priorities. Work very hard at building relationships to gain that respect and trust of people, because in the COO role it is all about the respect and the trust of the people that work for you. That will feature prominently in your ability to achieve the corporation's goals. Communication and transparency are just critical to making these relationships—upwards and downwards—work.

Managing the Organizational Hierarchy and Conveying Authority

A third key element of the CEO-COO relationship that our respondents spoke to repeatedly concerned maintaining the right amount of hierarchy between the two positions. On the one extreme are the examples of the two-in-a-box approach, where the individuals are as close to equal in authority as is possible. On the other extreme are cases where the COO is clearly subordinate to the CEO. More generally, a key feature of the COO role is the notion of having to simultaneously be a loyal follower to the CEO while also serving as a strong leader to others in the organization. When we raised this point with Bob Herbold, former COO at Microsoft, he responded:

> You are onto something really important that often leads to disaster if it is not nailed down. To me, this is a key, key issue and the way it gets worked out is the individuals, through trial and error, as well as through discussions, figure out who is going to be doing what and who needs to check with who on key decisions. There are some instances where confidence will be developed and the individual goes off and just does things. There will be other instances where the decision is sensitive enough that both parties want to be exposed to it and how the team will make that happen needs to be agreed to very early in the relationship.

Boundaries

A fourth element of the CEO-COO relationship regards concern for any COO who does not obtain up-front a clear idea of where the boundaries are between his or her areas of responsibility and those of the CEO. It is far easier to delineate boundaries when the number one and two clearly have complementary competencies and each naturally gravitates to areas of expertise. The more their competencies overlap, the greater the likelihood that the COO might feel (perhaps accurately) that the CEO is inclined to micromanage some areas and second-guess decisions in other areas. These behaviors on the part of the CEO certainly communicate to the COO a lack of trust, which likely will engender friction in the relationship. Logically, then, an important consideration in creating the CEO-COO structure is ensuring that the executives complement one another through their competencies. Too much overlap invites micromanagement and dissension; too little overlap may result in a competency gap that disadvantages the entire company. Over time, the company will evolve; members of the top management team develop and turn over. Consequently, the boundaries between their roles need to change. For example, Maynard Webb, COO at eBay, noted that the role there varied with the strengths of the incumbent:

> I am the second COO at eBay. The first COO, Brian Swette, had a job that was nothing like my job. At the time, the three of us ran eBay—it would be Meg, Brian, and me. Brian was a sales and marketing guy. He had the business units reporting directly to him and spent no time on any of my role. It was more like three in a box, if you will.

Further, Del Yocam, who served as COO at Apple Computer, talked about how important it was for him to have a clear line of demarcation between his job and the CEO's job:

> As COO, I wanted to understand what my responsibility versus that of the CEO is. John [Sculley] and I were able to do that very early on. His role was strategic direction of the company, the strategic plan, the external relations—whether they're with shareholders, industry pundits, acquisitions. My job was the operating plan, the running of the company, the annual business planning process. I ran the company on a day-by-day, month-by-month, quarter-by-quarter basis. You have to have those defined responsibilities up front to make sure that you're able to do your job. In our case, that was clearly done—and done early on.

Similarly, Bill Swanson (currently the CEO at Raytheon) described his thinking about the COO position when he was offered the position by then-CEO Dan Burnham:

> The first thing to understand when evaluating such a position is to make sure the roles and responsibilities are defined. I would tell any deputy or CEO, if you go into a job and you don't know your four corners, don't take it. . . . The second key is to make sure everyone else understands how the COO and CEO are splitting work. We made things clear so that there wasn't an overlap. Spending the time defining the roles and responsibilities is very important. We also agreed that if he made a call, that was the call—and if I made the call, then that was the call. Unless I had done something really stupid, he agreed to back my decision. Similarly, I had to respect the fact that he was in charge and there would be times when it was his decision even though I didn't agree. Finally, another thing that was absolutely key is that regularly Dan and I would either chat or e-mail or phone and let each kind of know what the key points were so somebody couldn't back-door with a "he said, you said" kind of thing. We were pretty good about that. Together you have to communicate frequently and maintain your alignment on the key issues. Dan and I made sure that we kept each other informed.

In one interview with an executive who had experience with an unsuccessful stint as COO, the boundary issue was the fatal flaw. Essentially, the COO was faced with a situation where the CEO was not willing to cede responsibilities. This suggests that it is one thing to have an agreement as to where one job ends and another begins, but as is the case with so much in business today effective execution of the plan matters.

Relationships with Other Members of Top Management

In creating a COO role, management is making a major structural change to the form of the organization. Specifically, creating the COO role adds a layer to management. Generally, organizations turn responsibility for all areas of operations over to the COO; this typically includes production and manufacturing, marketing and sales, and research and development. Individuals heading these functions may previously have had direct access to the CEO and now have an intermediary to address. One of the COO's first challenges is to develop relationships with direct reports that discourage them from seeking back-door access to the CEO. Similarly, COOs count on the CEO to support their position and block efforts by those who might want to circumvent the COO. A number of the people we interviewed commented on how critical it is for the CEO especially to have a great deal of personal discipline in this area so that a back door never opens up. This is not to say that restricting access to the CEO is the goal. In fact, most of the CEOs and COOs commented that they both encouraged an open-door policy with all of the executives. The important factor instead is that decisions need to be made where advertised and then supported publicly and privately. A number of them also commented that even when they disagreed, they kept the public appearance and stood shoulder to shoulder until they had time together to privately consider the issue. We are not arguing that the CEO should abolish ties to the broader leadership team; our position is quite to the contrary. The CEO needs to stay connected and accessible to the leadership team and the business; however, he or she must refrain from making or second-guessing decisions that clearly fall under the COO. Instead, the CEO needs to push people back to the number two whenever it is appropriate. Of course, the COO needs to be effective at establishing strong working relationships with those members of top management who remain as direct reports to the CEO. The challenges in managing these relationships were succinctly summarized by Webb at eBay:

> I have been working on nailing that back door shut for a while. I think it is a tough, tough thing to do, especially when you have a CEO that actually loves to get involved in problem solving and wants to help. I think what you have to do in that case is to enable, not control, communication and be transparent. At the same time, you have to be willing to be strong enough to still step up and do the things you need to do. I will tell you it is an art, not a science. It is very hard.

Relationship with the Board

Most of the COOs we spoke to had regular access to the board and often attended the majority of board meetings. For example, Webb told us that access to the board is critical for the success of the COO. At eBay, he drives the work of the compensation committee and is a key member of the governance committee. Additionally, he has been part of the board's discussions about succession planning at eBay. The issue that arises by being an insider and potential successor is that the board sees the good, the bad, and the ugly around how the CEO and COO have exercised leadership and approached execution of the business strategy. No matter how competent an executive is, there will always be missteps and missed opportunities that are remembered. Many COOs notice that it is difficult in that position to be recognized for their contribution because of the long shadow cast by the CEO. In some ways, the COO job is to make the CEO successful; in doing so, the COO in some ways lessens his or her apparent contribution. If the CEO is not conscientious about efforts to make sure credit is attributed to others, the impression the board has of the number two will not be enhanced. CEOs concerned with the ultimate promotability of their number two need to be deliberate about their efforts, whenever appropriate, to share the spotlight.

Additionally, the COO has to overcome the tendency of people to put someone in a box, in this case the COO box. For some, it is difficult to get out of it. Perhaps this is why you do see a COO becoming CEO at a company other than the one the person grew up in. When it comes time for the succession plan to be enacted, the board members may only remember the bad and the ugly, causing them to go outside for a suitable replacement for the CEO. People coming in from the outside are well positioned without any warts and often look flawless in their careers.

Keeping Your Ego in Check

We repeatedly heard how critical it is for the number two to check his or her ego at the door. As Harry Levinson said, the COO must "recognize and accept the fact that his or her major task is making the number one look good. . . . It is as a piano accompanist to a violin soloist."[4] The ability to work tirelessly to lead and execute in support of a strategy that brings accolades to another will frustrate someone who cannot sublimate his or her own ego—at least for the period of time spent serving as COO. As Maynard Webb said,

> Low ego need is a big deal in the COO role. You have to lead while serving. It has been the hardest job that I have ever done, and because it is not as immediate with gratification as any of the line jobs that I had. When you are solving technology issues, such as, "Is the site up or not?" it is pretty black-and-white. You see some of the results pretty quickly, but you are working on things through a lot more layers as COO and the results come much slower.

Not only do the results come more slowly—or in a way that makes attribution for the outcome more difficult to discern—but the COO is not necessarily in line to receive the kudos if the job was well done. Executives shared with us the frustration that comes with serving as a COO to someone Jim Collins would say has not developed the capabilities of a level-five leader—that is, someone who deliberately looks for others to apportion credit.[5]

Career Aspirations

COOs need to understand how strong their desire is to be the number one. This is important for several reasons. First, even CEO-COO pairings that might be described as a healthy mentor-protégé relationship can run as such for only a limited time. Second, when a COO realizes he or she is ready for a step up, the temptation to overreach his or her own authority grows and could result in a misstep. As Ed Zander told us about his time working with Scott McNealy at Sun Microsystems, when the CEO and COO begin to diverge on their thoughts about the best strategy to take the company forward, it is time for the COO to move on. Observers and some of the executives we interviewed commented on that after some period of time as a number two the COO may begin to be viewed as plateaued—unable to move from a position that executes a strategy to a position that leads in developing strategy.[6] Finally, the COO faces a real challenge when a new CEO is brought in from outside the firm. Barbara Ettore describes the COO as "instantly disenchanted" and ripe for the picking by competitors.[7] This circumstance is intuitive, and both the firm and the COO incumbent should be in a position to manage through it. That said, we have previously cited a number of examples of talent lost as a result of how the CEO succession was managed.

SUMMARY

In this chapter, we introduced three categories of COO positions: those where the incumbent predominantly operates inside the firm, working to manage either a particular initiative or day-to-day operations; those individuals brought in to create a partnership with the CEO, often characterized by an amorphous division of labor between the two; and those labeled situational—in other words, those not falling neatly into either category because the nature of the position seemed determined by idiosyncrasies of the focal company, its context, and its strategy. An important point in regard to staffing the position emerges from understanding which of the three is salient. In the first case, deep industry knowledge, credibility with employees, and the ability to quickly size up and respond to existing challenges are critical competencies. In the second, the more critical dimension on which to assess a candidate is demonstrated or likely ability to quickly get in step with the CEO to ensure seamlessness in their relationship, their vision, and their communication inside and outside the company. Of course, the final case is the most difficult for making a definitive statement because the characteristics that determine fit are so particular to the situation. Consequently, boards and executives of these organizations are advised to carefully diagnose the situation and develop shared understanding as to the objectives sought through selection of a COO in order to properly begin the search process.

In addition, a number of challenges that new COOs are likely to face were discussed. Obviously, like any other new manager, COOs need to be confident in their ability to develop effective working relationships with their reports. Similarly, this sentiment has to exist regarding their colleagues on the top management team. An added complexity is introduced where the COO position is new and alters reporting relationships for other members of that team. COOs have to be skilled at understanding how to best manage the way their direct reports experience relating to the CEO, the person to whom they formerly reported. As noted by our respondents, there is an art to this; mastery is part of what makes an effective COO special.

Two final and somewhat interrelated points were raised, concerning the COO's need to sublimate his or her own ego and the importance for the COO of understanding how instrumental this position is with regard to career aspirations. Incumbents need to remember they are COO; those who overstretch inevitably end up in an uncomfortable situation. Similarly, if the COO needs public recognition of one form or another to feel validated in the role, he or she is liable to quickly become frustrated working under any but the most modest CEO. Finally, do the COO, the CEO, the board, and all other relevant parties share an understanding of the circumstances—if any—under which this COO position might lead to an opportunity to lead the firm as CEO?

Inconsistency or misunderstanding here does not bode well for the long-term satisfaction of the COO or the effectiveness of the CEO-COO partnership.

NOTES

1. Hambrick, D. C., and A. A. Cannella, Jr. 2004. Ceos who have Coos: Contingency analysis of an unexplored structural form. *Strategic Management Journal, 25,* 959–980.
2. Henry Mintzberg, quoted in Hambrick and Cannella (2004).
3. Robbins, S. P. 2004. *Essentials of organizational behavior* (7th ed.). Upper Saddle River, NJ: Prentice Hall.
4. Harry Levinson, quoted in Ettore, B. 1993. Who is this person? Focus on the number two. *Management Review, 82*(2).
5. Collins, J. 2001. *Good to great.* New York: Harper.
6. Hymowitz, C. 2004, August 10. Executives in no. 2 job shouldn't bide time for too many years. *Wall Street Journal,* Sect. B1.
7. Ettore (1993).

A CONVERSATION WITH JOE LEONARD

CHAIRMAN OF THE BOARD AND CEO, AIRTRAN AIRWAYS
FORMERLY COO, EASTERN AIRLINES

Joe Leonard is chairman and chief executive officer of AirTran Holdings and its subsidiary, AirTran Airways. A thirty-year industry veteran, he joined AirTran Airways in January 1999. Prior to coming to AirTran, he served as president and CEO of Allied Signal's aerospace marketing, sales, and service organization. Before joining Allied Signal, he held positions that included COO for Eastern Air Lines as well as a number of key management positions at American Airlines, Northwest Airlines, and Boeing (http://www.airtran.com/aboutus/investor/index.jsp).

AUTHORS: You recently decided to create a COO position at AirTran. What can you tell us about that process?

LEONARD: In our particular situation, we had to just about completely rebuild the management team. Since we had a lot of work to do, we needed more hands on deck, so to speak. I think in the long term we probably will not have a senior VP of operations (Steven Kolski) and a COO (Robert Fornaro), which we currently have today. But for now, because we have so much work to do, we need both positions. In our case, our COO, Bob, has a skill set and experiences that are different from mine. I think it's likely as a result that one plus one is more than two. He has a background in planning and in marketing, and my background is in operations and labor and working with the FAA. I think the combination of our two skill sets hopefully ends up creating something great. If the skill sets are too similar, that brings no value to the firm.

AUTHORS: How does your leadership team make decisions? How would you describe the relationships among the team members?

LEONARD: The way we try to manage is on a collegial basis. We have a very simple structure, a very flat structure. We try to get everyone's varied input—and it is not too hard because all I have to do is stick my head out the door and say, "Guys, come over"—and we can hold an impromptu meeting and make a pretty quick decision. I think it helps with the learning for everybody to get everybody's input as well.

In all, I am trying to encourage co-leadership. I think we do a pretty decent job of that. As time has gone on, I have made a deliberate effort to back out at times—because if I am willing to make every decision, everybody will come to me—there is no doubt about that. I think CEOs have to make an effort to back away, because if they don't then the number two guy is never going to get his feet on the ground. It is something you have to be cognizant of, one; and want to happen, two; and three, work at, because most CEOs are A-type personalities and this letting go is not something easy to do.

AUTHORS: What about the way you divide up the direct reports in your case? Who gets who?

LEONARD: At AirTran, Bob reports to me and everybody else reports to him. I have no problems walking the hall and talking to some junior manager about something. Bob has no qualms about doing the same thing. As best we can, we try to make sure there are no lines in the company, and again, we have a formal staff meeting once a week—we only have one a week. That is a regularly scheduled meeting. We require everyone to come down Monday morning for that meeting so that at least once a week everybody is in one room at the same time.

We make sure that whatever is on people's minds it is surfaced at that meeting. If somebody comes in Tuesday and says, "I have something to talk about that affects this other guy's area" the almost immediate response is, "Why the hell didn't you bring it up yesterday when he was here?" We are pretty disciplined about that.

AUTHORS: **What is it about your relationship with Bob that allows this co-leadership model, and this flat structure, to work so well?**

LEONARD: I think there is a mutual respect, in our case, for certain. I had met Bob back at Northwest in 1991 and though we didn't work together that long we knew each other and respected each other. The day it was announced that I was leaving Allied Signal to come here, Bob and I talked about him joining me down here, and he came down. I still tease him about being risk-averse because he wouldn't sign up right away, and came down on a consulting basis for a couple of months and then joined the company.

AUTHORS: **Were there issues bringing an outsider in as a number two? Was there a lot of friction and tension?**

LEONARD: I think he fit in real well. The company was in desperate trouble and you don't really have time to worry about some of those other things when you are in that kind of condition. I describe it as, we were on cash fumes at the time.

AUTHORS: **Arguably, with Bob and the rest of the leadership team, you guys led one of the best turnarounds in terms of where you were to where you are today. It has been quite a remarkable achievement.**

LEONARD: Credit clearly belongs to the whole team. I think everybody respects one another. If somebody steps out of line, somebody else usually swings by their office at the end of the day and says, "That's really not the way we do things around here." We brought in a lot of guys who had been around a long time, who knew what to do. I think one of the advantages we have as a company is we have people who know what to do and can make command decisions and move fast. And we have some young guys coming up that are very, very good. Our maintenance guy is pretty young for being the senior maintenance guy. Our flight operations VP is very young for his job.

So we have some pretty young guys too. We have some folks that have been around, and have been through bad situations. I think you learn a lot more when you have been through bad situations than you do when everything is running on all eight cylinders.

And trust builds and relationships build, and you sort of get the glue that makes it work afterwards too, which many people—if you bring people in when it is running on all cylinders, you may get the politics and all the ancillary stuff that doesn't add any value.

AUTHORS: **When you were looking for a number two, was there a set of skills you were looking for?**

LEONARD: **Well,** I was sort of looking for somebody that understood the revenue side of the business. I personally believe to this day that Bob Fornaro is the best in the industry at understanding how it works. There are a lot of guys in the industry that have been in it a long time who still don't understand the way he does. He has a mental picture of how things fit together and what will work and what won't. That was paramount because our revenue production was abysmal at the time. And I also knew Bob; Bob is a guy who has guts. I needed somebody that could stand up and move on. I remember early on one day he came in and said, "You know, nobody likes firing people, but you have to, especially in a turnaround," and he said, "This is the easiest place that has ever been for me to do that—the reason it is easy is because the stakes are so high. If we make a mistake, we are going to go out of business. If we tolerate guys who can't pull their weight, we are going to run this company out of business." Coming in to a more normal situation might allow you to spend months fretting over things like that. In that environment you just couldn't hesitate or you were putting *everybody's* job at risk. I needed a COO who could make those decisions.

AUTHORS: **What advice would you offer CEOs who are thinking about adding a number two? What things should they think about?**

LEONARD: I am a strong believer in, You build the organization around the personalities rather than vice versa. I think you have to take an assessment of who you've got, what the skill sets are, and then you fill and organize around that. I think organizations should be fluid. What works for a certain set of players may not work for another set of players. I think the organization should be fluid enough to recognize that. It is also true that what may be necessary at one stage of development may be totally inappropriate in another stage of development. If you look at our company size six years ago—when we came in—it was in a crisis. We needed crisis managers—people that just knew what to do and went and did it. Now this year we will be $1.3–1.4 billion in revenue; we are four times our previous size; we will have seven thousand employees versus two thousand and so the needs are quite a bit different. We are focusing a lot more on management development and those kinds of things than we did a few years ago where we simply didn't have time for that. I really very strongly believe that the structure has to be fluid and fit with the personalities and needs of the organization.

AUTHORS: A number of airlines have created the COO position. What are your thoughts on why that is the case?

LEONARD: I think the complexity of the business, the challenges the industry faces—and for us, the speed of growth—has a lot to do with it. I think the requirements outside of the company had a lot to do with it, too. For instance, I tend to handle the Washington area, and I tend to handle the press and things like that. Bob and I have split things into an inside and an outside job, so to speak. I think airlines tend to get a disproportionate amount of attention from the press and the government, more than we probably deserve, but it is just a fact of life. So creating a number two in order to free the CEO up to manage those external constituents makes logical sense. At Allied Signal, when I was there, there were three number twos. . . . You had Larry Bossidy, our chairman, and we didn't have a COO, but we had three sector presidents who ran the separate businesses. I thought that worked pretty well in that environment. Again, a lot has to do with the personalities. I don't think Larry would have felt comfortable with a COO.

AUTHORS: How well does the number two set you up to be the number one?

LEONARD: It should, though success as a number two does not guarantee success as a CEO. I don't think it is ever a guarantee, especially with the pressures put on management these days to meet quarterly results in this, that, and the other. Clearly in our case, we are trying to build bench strength, and certainly I am doing everything I know how to make sure when I depart here that Bob will be considered as the guy that ought to lead the company to the next challenge. We are doing a really good job at building bench strength underneath that as well. I mean, one of the things we do at our board meetings is we have one of our division leaders make a presentation to the board on what they are doing so they can get exposure to the board and start identifying who could run this place down the road. I think we have some guys lined up that can run this place.

AUTHORS: Is there a life span to the number two, or can it go on forever?

LEONARD: Absolutely. I believe there is a life span for the number one and the number two—probably more so for the number one than the number two. I am one that doesn't believe that CEOs in particular should hang around forever, and if you are a number two guy you will probably get stale faster. I think people do get stale; I think you do need challenges. I think you need change. I remember I told one of my ex-bosses who I admire immensely, I said, "I think CEOs are good for about seven years." He said, "So in other words, the last eighteen years of my career were a waste of time." I didn't exactly mean it that way! I think those days are kind of over, not completely, but generally speaking. You don't see many CEOs sticking around for twenty-five years anymore.

A CONVERSATION WITH FRED POSES

CHAIRMAN AND CEO, AMERICAN STANDARD COMPANIES
FORMERLY COO, ALLIED SIGNAL

Fred Poses has been chairman and chief executive officer of American Standard Companies since January 2000. Prior to joining American Standard, he served as president and COO of Allied Signal. He originally joined Allied Signal in 1969 as a financial analyst. In more than thirty years with the company, he served in a number of positions with increasing responsibility and ultimately was named president of the engineered materials sector and EVP of the corporation in 1988. In October 1997, he was elected to the board of directors and named vice chairman of Allied Signal. He was appointed president and COO in June 1998 (http://ir.americanstandard.com/mgmt-detail.cfm?id=693).

AUTHORS: What from your experience as COO at Allied Signal stands out to you today?

POSES: As the COO, I worked for a CEO [Larry Bossidy] who was very engaged in both the strategic direction and the day-to-day operations of the company. Some COOs find themselves working for a CEO who views himself as a strategy guy, maybe a Mr. Outside. In those situations, the CEO primarily works with the board, analysts, and others outside the firm. He turns over the day-to-day operations of the company to the COO. That wasn't the world I lived in at Allied Signal. We operated as a team, rather than having distinct roles. As part of that partnership, I took a leadership role on certain strategic initiatives. For example, I led the initiative to accelerate our growth opportunities. Larry knew that growth was important to the company, and he essentially told me, "You go lead that."

AUTHORS: How would you describe your relationship with Larry as CEO? Was it a typical CEO-COO relationship?

POSES: I am not sure what's "typical." I'm sure you will find lots of models, but in part I see the COO as another set of eyes, another set of ears, and another voice—a person who sometimes advocates a different point of view. In a good CEO-COO relationship, you have to be able to argue, to debate—even to fight when that's necessary. So Larry and I would battle sometimes, not to see who would win or lose but to see how we could make the company better. We certainly had our fair share of heated discussions, but I think that's what he wanted. We could do that because we both trusted that the other was fighting for what he thought was best for Allied Signal.

AUTHORS: What words of warning would you give someone considering a COO job?

POSES: First, I would encourage that person to pose some basic questions. What are the roles and responsibilities of the COO? Does the CEO really want a COO, or is the board forcing him? Is the CEO creating a COO because there are things that may be right for the company but he just doesn't want to do them? In situations like that, the new COO gets stuck with a funny agenda and no support. I don't know the COO batting average in terms of job success, but I wouldn't be surprised if it's pretty low.

In the end, if you don't design the COO role around a real business need, I'd bet that the business underperforms and the COO is labeled a failure. In some firms, the COO job is a bit of a testing role—the board wants to see if this person is CEO material. In some instances, firms face such a difficult external environment—bankruptcy, asbestos litigation, corporate governance problems, big environmental issues—that the CEO doesn't have time to handle the people and run the business, no matter the size of the business. Under those conditions, having a COO position makes sense. It also makes sense in firms undertaking a big strategic change. For example, suppose American Standard made buses and decided that we also wanted to make airplanes. That would require a big transition, a completely different focus and a completely different energy. But while we were pursuing the airplane business, we couldn't let the wheels fall off our buses. In a big strategic shift like that, the CEO and COO can logically divide up responsibility for launching the new business and for running the existing business.

To return more directly to your question, I think the prospective COO needs to ask himself or herself, "What am I going to get from this experience?" I was lucky to have been number two to a great number one. So I learned a lot. I always have said that working for Larry made me a better leader and made my transition to American Standard CEO much easier.

Looking back on the experience, one of the things I most appreciate is that Larry let me be me. He accepted who I was and left me free to think independently. The company was big enough that I could set my priorities and create a leadership position where I could experiment. I wasn't just learning from Larry, but I was also learning from my own successes and failures. That is a critical thing for COOs—first-hand experience makes you a much sharper judge of what it takes to succeed.

AUTHORS: Talk about your transition from the number two to the number one. What, in your mind, were the surprises?

POSES: Because of my experience working as COO, I was well-prepared to step into the role, and there were fewer surprises than I expected. The biggest surprise was that I could create my own agenda. Despite all the freedom I had at Allied Signal, I couldn't set an agenda for the whole company to follow. That's the CEO's role. Through my experience as COO to Larry, I saw the power of leadership. I saw the power of a consistent agenda. I saw the power of setting higher standards by raising expectations. And I came to appreciate the value of communication. Without that experience, I don't think I would have understood the power of these things when I came to American Standard.

My experience as COO at Allied Signal also taught me valuable lessons about recognizing and working with talented people. If you have never played on a winning team with great talent, how do you learn to know what a talented team looks like? Working for Larry, who had thirty-plus years with GE, was very helpful. He came with a high set of standards and built on what he had learned, applying his knowledge to Allied's needs. You can learn a lot from your previous company—and, in my case, from your CEO's previous company—that you can apply when you take on a CEO position. Larry's role as an outsider CEO who became very successful also prepared me for my own transition from Allied COO to American Standard CEO.

When I looked for a new opportunity, I wanted a CEO position where my experience would be relevant—not just leadership experience, but industry experience too. I felt very comfortable going from one industrial company to another. Some executives have made the switch from industrial to retail companies, for instance, and been very successful at it. In making a transition like that, though, you have much more of a learning curve as you adjust to a new industry.

AUTHORS: What did it take for you to become more comfortable with the external pieces of the number one role—dealing with the board, analysts, and so on?

POSES: I would add that Larry did a good job there also. While he was there—even before I became a board member—I always went to the board meetings. Our board meetings were open. It was not one of those situations where you come in, give your presentation and then leave the room. I was always there to listen and learn. I had the benefit of not only working with the board, but also getting to know them socially a bit. When you realize they are "people"—they have seen problems and opportunities before, they have families and kids, and they are not perfect either—the relationship becomes less intimidating. The board interaction I had at Allied Signal was invaluable in preparing me to build a good working relationship with the board at American Standard when I became CEO.

AUTHORS: How long can someone effectively serve as a number two?

POSES: You know, I'm a funny guy. I never found a job I wanted to leave. There was one point in my Allied Signal career—before Larry was there—when I was offered a different job. It was a "better" job, but I didn't want to leave. I liked what I was doing, I liked the people I was working with, and we were doing great things. So I stayed. On the other hand, there are some people who are constantly plotting their career. I don't know where they got this gene, but it seems that they are plotting from the playpen until they become chairman and CEO. I think number twos can get themselves in trouble if they become dissatisfied with their current job because they are too obsessed with what the next job might be. Number twos do themselves and their companies a disservice if they act as if "I am going to get the number one job," or "Oh boy, if I don't get this in two years, I'm out of here" or "I'm just biding my time until I get that number one job." No one wants to work with or for that person. People want to be part of a team that is focused on the company's success, not on the success of one individual. One of the surest signs of failure is an overly ambitious, number one wannabe. Those individuals are not willing to do what it takes to accomplish what needs to be done today, because they're too focused on their future. I always have felt that if I do a good job, the future will take care of itself.

A CONVERSATION WITH STEVEN REINEMUND

CHAIRMAN OF THE BOARD AND CEO, PEPSICO
FORMERLY PRESIDENT AND COO OF PEPSICO

Steven Reinemund has been PepsiCo's chairman and chief executive officer since May 2001. From September 1999 until that appointment, he served as PepsiCo's president and chief operating officer. Reinemund began his career with PepsiCo in 1984 as a senior operating officer of Pizza Hut. He became president and CEO of Pizza Hut in 1986, and of Pizza Hut Worldwide in 1991. In 1992, Reinemund became president and chief executive officer of Frito-Lay and chairman and CEO in 1996. He is also a director of Johnson and Johnson (http://www.pepsico.com/company/directors-committees.shtml#Reinemund).

AUTHORS: Is there a time when it makes sense to have a COO?

REINEMUND: I think there has to be a real particular reason to have a COO. When a company is very clear as to what the reason is, then the role makes a lot of sense. If it is not clear, or if ultimately the reason behind the position is really not a good reason, then that is a problem. For instance, if the CEO is just looking to lessen his work load, it is not a good reason. There can be a lot of reasons why a COO position is created. One is because the strategic demands of the business require more than one person, or it is a developmental opportunity for someone; the company wants to see them from a different light. I don't necessarily believe that someone has to be in that role in order to become a CEO, but if there is a particular question about an individual's ability to do a certain aspect of what you think a CEO should do, it is a good way to test them. Many of us who grew up running businesses like it. It is a fun job. It is a hands-on job. You get to mold the strategy; you get to direct the efforts every day. You have the functional people that you work with and that team performs against a mission and it is an exciting experience. Not everybody who does that job wants to do a different kind of job, and frankly speaking, for myself I had to wrestle as to whether I really wanted to do anything other than run a division or a single business. For several years, I basically resisted making that move. But if a board wants to see if an individual can step out of doing day-to-day, hands-on directing and leading of a business and direct and teach and coach others—all of which are part of a CEO's job—then it is worth trying to put them in a COO job to test them.

AUTHORS: When you went into the COO role at PepsiCo—granted it was for a reasonably short period of time—did it prepare you well to be CEO?

REINEMUND: Absolutely. It was very worthwhile, on a number of fronts. One, strategically we were going through some transitions, including a merger and an acquisition, and it really made it a whole lot easier to have that structure. Secondly, I think frankly the board probably wanted to see if I could step out of being a division president and that was probably a large part of it. There was a succession plan in place—no guarantee on it, but that was part of it too.

AUTHORS: What about changes in your relationship with the CEO? How did that work in terms of sharing of decision making and power?

REINEMUND: I can tell you from the time Roger [Enrico] asked me to do the job to now, we never, ever had a rough spot. That may sound naïve, but I think it is because Roger clearly defined what the role was and what it wasn't. If both parties understand that, then it works. Many times, the CEO is not disciplined enough to stick to what they laid out as the role.

AUTHORS: What was the biggest surprise when you moved up into the CEO role yourself?

REINEMUND: Frankly, the biggest surprises were gradual, not something that just jumps out. Also, the external environment changed around me. I came in May 2001, there was September 11, and then Enron and all the other corporate governance issues and Sarbanes Oxley and everything. I probably came in at a unique time. In fact there are several of us who came into the CEO role right around the same time, and we get together from time to time to talk about our lives versus our predecessors' lives. I think it would have been pretty difficult to transition from some of our predecessors, to life today where the world is just very different.

AUTHORS: It seems larger companies like PepsiCo use the divisional structure rather than a single clear number two to develop the next generation of CEO candidates. Would you talk a little bit about what it was like for you moving from the position as a divisional CEO into this role as CEO?

REINEMUND: I had to think long and hard about whether I wanted to really move out of running the day-to-day business into a role where I coach and coordinate. I think it first starts with recognizing there is a difference and deciding you want to do something different, and then recognizing that you have to work at it. For the people who have done it a long time, it is hard to make that transition, at least for a lot of us it is.

AUTHORS: What about the skill sets of the CEO and COO? Do you need overlap?

REINEMUND: If there is a whole lot of overlap you have to decide whether there is a reason for the two jobs. In fact, I would submit that if there is a lot of overlap, there isn't a need for both jobs. When Roger and I worked together, he clearly assigned me the coordination and direction of the day-to-day business.

He was very clear that he wasn't going to get involved in that—and he didn't initiate it, and he never allowed others to consciously or subconsciously draw him into it either. He was very consistent.

AUTHORS: Was coming in to the number two job as an insider an advantage or a disadvantage?

REINEMUND: You have different advantages and disadvantages whether you are an insider or outsider. As an insider, people know you, both for good and for bad. When you come in from outside, they don't know or have as much information. If an organization makes a selection and the insiders reject the candidate, you are going to know it pretty quickly. What happens many times is the CEO makes that selection and then they don't have the strength of will to stand behind it and make it work, because there are going to be people that are going to test it and they have to be very consistent to stand behind it.

AUTHORS: How would you evaluate whether a COO has been effective or not?

REINEMUND: I think you have answered it. You have to answer it in the context of why you have it. There are differences in the motivations behind the creation of the role, and then there are differences in the way the role is shaped. It is so often tailored to the capabilities of the individual. If you are using it to try to develop someone, you might look at where it is that we need to do that development, or perhaps where they have some strengths we think we can leverage to help the company. The company down the street could be making a decision to put a COO in place and come up with a role that looks absolutely different. There are so many people who think they are going to make their lives easier by putting a COO in without any more reason—that will end up almost always being a bad decision. Certainly short-term for the CEO, bringing somebody on board in the number two position is actually going to create work; it is not going to free time. If you want to turn them into an effective executive, you are going to have to make an investment.

AUTHORS: If a colleague of yours was offered a position as a COO someplace, what would you encourage him or her to be careful about before taking the job?

REINEMUND: Make sure you understand what the job is and why it is. If it is simply to come in to be an understudy as a potential for succession, and there is nothing more to it than that, I would be very skeptical from an outsider's perspective. I think it is a high potential for failure.

AUTHORS: **There seems to be a consensus that it is a very difficult role for an outsider to do.**

REINEMUND: If you think about the very nature of what a chief operating officer's role is, regardless of why they are in that role, an outsider inherently comes with a disadvantage. My perspective is that the more senior the person you hire, the more important it is to bring a person in who brings something to the party that the organization doesn't have, so they can bring that to the party while they get enough runway to learn what the organization is all about. That was certainly my case when I came into Pizza Hut. I came in with one set of skills that the organization didn't have, and I was short on a lot of skills the organization did have, but that marriage worked. When you come in and you don't have that, it is hard. If you think about a chief operating officer's role, the role is to maximize the performance of the organization. You are not involved or responsible for the strategy—that is the CEO and the division president. You are responsible for coordinating, coaching, and maximizing, and frankly, if you—as COO—have no experience in the company, you are bringing nothing to the party. It is really tough.

A CONVERSATION WITH KEVIN SHARER

CEO, AMGEN
FORMERLY PRESIDENT AND COO, AMGEN

Kevin Sharer has served as a director of Amgen since November 1992. From October 1992 to May 2000, Sharer served as president and COO of the company. Since May 2000, he has been chief executive officer and president of the company. He was named chairman of the board in December 2000. Before joining Amgen, he served as president of the Business Markets Division of MCI Communications, a telecommunications

company. From February 1984 to March 1989, Sharer held numerous executive positions at General Electric (http://www.amgen.com/investors/leadership_team.html).

AUTHORS: Tell us what you see as critical in terms of the CEO-COO
relationship.

SHARER: First, I'd like to say that I think Gordon Binder [former Amgen
CEO] and I had a really, really good partnership. We were close to an ideal
number one, number two combination. It wasn't perfect, nothing in human
affairs is, but we were an effective team. We have dramatically different personal styles, which I think was good, but we had a very common set of beliefs
about the mission of the company, the strategy, our personal values, and so
on. So the first thing is, if the top two guys don't have that, there is a problem.
The second thing is that the success of the partnership is 75 percent dependent upon a few things that the CEO does—which I will talk about—and
probably 25 percent on whether or not the number two guy really, really has
the skill and humility to understand he is the number two guy and must support the boss.

The 75 percent the CEO creates—does the CEO give the number two person space? Does he actually give the number two person real authority, real
operating responsibility, power that is real, power that is seen by the rest of
the company as real? Second thing is, Does the number one guy actually encourage and let the number two person have his or her own voice in board
meetings and operating reviews? Can they actually sound like an independent
person? Number three, does the top guy give coaching, counseling, and really
see the success of number two as part of the company's success and encourage
the number two along to eventually become number one? And does he have
a mentor kind of relationship? These things are really hard to do, and I think
that is a lot of why it usually doesn't work.

The 25 percent, for the number two person, is, Do you have the humility
to know you are not number one? Both Gordon and I were ex-Navy guys. We
understood implicitly—we never talked about it, but we understood implicitly what the difference is between captain and executive officer. The executive officer on the ship is the number two guy. We just knew those roles; we

learned them when we were in our twenties and it is good model. Sometimes the number two guy can be the enforcer and make the captain look good. And the number two person keeps their counsel to the CEO private. There is none of this backbiting and what have you, and the number two person has to be patient. Any number two person worth their salt knows they are better than the number one—at least until you actually get the job and you find out, "This is harder than I thought"!

The relationship is really easy to describe, but boy, is it hard to do. A lot of the most important things in life fit in that category: easy to describe, hard to do. I give enormous credit to Gordon Binder. He gave me lots of leeway, I was on the board from the get go, he let me have my own relationships with board members; I just can't say enough about how much room Gordon gave me to have a fulfilling time. In retrospect, he was a heck of a guy for doing that. I think for me, I deserve some modest credit for understanding I was a number two and trying to advance the company and not my own personal agenda.

AUTHORS: You succeeded Gordon as CEO. As you transitioned to the number one job, what was missing from your learning in the number two job?

SHARER: Nothing. I was here seven years, I was on the board for those seven years, and so I had a very unusual preparation. I was prepared to be number one. There was no gap. It isn't that I didn't learn things as a CEO—I did, but it was not because I missed something when I was number two. It was about as seamless a transition as you could possibly have.

AUTHORS: What about the length of time as the number two? Had you imagined being COO for seven years?

SHARER: I think it is very individual and circumstantially specific. If you had said to me, "Hey, Kevin, you are going to be the number two guy for seven years" at the outset, I would have said there is about a 1 percent chance I will stay put. But the fact is, Gordon was good enough to me and the company was exciting enough, it made staying that length of time fine. But if you had to name a time, I think if you go over five years you are in the danger zone because a good number two is going to get frustrated. And if they are good, they are going to get picked off.

AUTHORS: What about reporting relationships? What you own, what reports to the COO versus the CEO?

SHARER: I think it is vital that the number two person have closure around something that is meaningful. In our case, I had closure around sales, marketing, engineering, manufacturing, construction. Gordon and I shared, literally shared, the CFO and the HR person. They reported to both of us. That wasn't the case from day one, but pretty soon that is the way it worked. We became very seamless in that sense. That was a real generous move by Gordon. Gordon had directly reporting to him our political operations, research, development, and law.

AUTHORS: Were there any shaping moments when you were in the COO job that have stayed with you?

SHARER: I think a couple. We had two crises early in my tenure. One was a crisis in China where we had some product government relationship problems; another was a supply crisis when we had an inventory problem. In both cases, Gordon let me handle them. He communicated to me enormous trust in that act and I really, really appreciated it. That stuff really, really stands out.

AUTHORS: Any advice for people who are becoming the number two?

SHARER: I think my advice would be to understand you are the number two and it is up to you to develop a good relationship with the number one. You need to be supportive of the boss, patient, but also have the skill to establish your own voice—and it is not easy to do.

A CONVERSATION WITH WILLIAM H. SWANSON

CHAIRMAN AND CEO, RAYTHEON

In January 2004, Bill Swanson added the responsibilities of chairman to his position as CEO of Raytheon. Prior to that, he was president of the company, responsible for Raytheon's government and defense operations, including the four strategic business areas of Missile Defense; Precision Engagement; Intelligence, Surveillance, and Reconnaissance; and Homeland Security. Prior to that assignment, he served as a Raytheon executive vice president and president of Electronic Systems. Swanson joined Raytheon in 1972 and has held a range of leadership positions. He is also the author of a little gray booklet called *Swanson's Unwritten Rules of Management* (http://www.raytheon.com/newsroom/stellent/groups/public/documents/legacy_site/cms01_052438.pdf).

AUTHORS: Having served as a number two and then rising to the CEO position, you are in a great position to talk about the two roles. To begin, please tell us a little about what you see as the keys to successfully managing the relationship between CEO and COO.

SWANSON: The first key is to clearly define the roles and responsibilities. For example, when Dan Burnham, our CEO at the time, called and asked me to be president, we talked about it a bit on the phone, but given the importance of the position I needed more information. So he said, "Why don't you put down on paper what you want to do?" And that was very helpful. I actually drafted an organization chart of reporting relationships. I felt it was pretty well defined and it created a useful framework for discussion. We agreed, for instance, that the government and defense businesses should report to me, but we had different ideas for the reporting structure for the corporate functions: finance, HR, communications, and so forth. Dan felt these functions should continue to report to him, while I felt that the number two individual in the leadership structure should report to the CEO, and that everybody else reported to the number two.

AUTHORS: Obviously, the story doesn't end there.

SWANSON: After thinking more about it, I didn't press the point, and in hindsight the reporting relationships worked just fine in practice. The functions wanted to understand my thinking, and we all worked well together. One shouldn't get overly concerned with structure on paper. More important is the actual role, the responsibilities, and how the organization functions. Whether a number two will be comfortable with this depends on his or her psyche. It worked well for Dan and me. Then again, we both made it work.

AUTHORS: So understanding what you are accepting responsibility for is key. What else comes to mind as critical in managing the CEO–COO relationship?

SWANSON: The second key is to make sure everyone understands how the COO and CEO are splitting the actual work. We made that very clear so that there was very minimal overlap. It is also important that the COO and CEO back each other up. Dan and I did that. We agreed that if he made a call, that was it—and if I made a call, the same thing. And I respected the fact that he was in charge and that there would be times when it was his decision, even though I might not agree. We also agreed that neither of us would talk about any differences of opinion we might have to members of our team; that would have undermined the effectiveness of the organization. And we were good about avoiding that. One other action that was absolutely key: We communicated with each other— face to face, by phone, or via e-mail—on key matters to discourage any "he said, you said" within the organization. We were very good about that.

AUTHORS: Do you think some friction—perhaps from the competitive spirit of the CEO and COO—is inevitable?

SWANSON: I think friction is avoided by putting the issues on the table. The friction is not a function of disagreeing with each other per se; there will always be disagreements. It's more a result of not airing the issues, of letting them fester. And I think we were good about discussing what was on our minds, and that prevented friction.

As for the competitive spirit, if the COO role is used properly then the organization will see the COO as the logical successor to the CEO and the team will start mentally preparing for the transition. Nevertheless, there will always be some concerns within an organization during leadership transition. I remember that when Dan announced his retirement, some people in our Six Sigma group worried about their future. Not only were their fears unfounded, I think everyone came to understand that I would be extremely supportive of Raytheon Six Sigma because I was a true believer, and I am. We still have the ultimate respect for Dan for starting Raytheon Six Sigma, but everybody realizes now that my passion for it is very real—and that I am unsympathetic to anyone who is not supportive of Six Sigma.

AUTHORS: Are the people in a number two position right to think of themselves as successors? Does that role properly develop someone to become CEO?

SWANSON: My strong view is that you should only have a number two if that number two is being developed. Like all organizations, we have had instances where we had to take people out of developmental positions because we realized they would not be leading their organizations. They may have been performing quite adequately in their current position, but the organizational goal was to groom them for a leadership role; so their current position needed to be developmental. If you move someone out of a developmental position, it is important to move someone else in as expeditiously as possible.

AUTHORS: They become a firm's asset.

SWANSON: Yes. When I have a deputy or COO or president, it will be because I am thinking of my transition, whenever that may be. And whoever is selected will need to be able to impress the board. At the level of president or COO, board dynamics are very important.

AUTHORS: What are the gaps that might remain in spite of the development a CEO tries to provide for the COO?

SWANSON: One never entirely knows if there will be a gap until the number two becomes CEO. An individual could be the best COO in the world, but when he or she becomes CEO, something could happen. One way to reduce the uncertainty is to develop a candidate internally. I often say that I will consider it a failure if my replacement comes from outside Raytheon. That doesn't mean we can't hire somebody from outside and have him or her spend four or five years with the company getting ready for the job; that's a different story. But the key is to make sure that we are developing our next leaders.

What has changed most for me in the transition from number two to CEO is that my priorities are so much different now. I am more involved in mentoring and teaching, more reflective and strategic. I love speaking to employee groups and drawing on their energy and making them feel energized as well. It feels so good to help people believe that this is truly *our* company and to treat the company's name as if it were their own. Communications is the number one priority because people have to receive and understand the message if they are to execute properly. You don't really appreciate that until you have the number one position. That wasn't my role as number two. Being number one is entirely, entirely different. What has been most gratifying is being able to tap into eighty thousand employees who truly believe that this is our time. This feeling, combined with a real need for our capabilities and a true focus within the company on performance, has helped us move toward our shared vision for Raytheon.

AUTHORS: Do you think there is a life span for a number two?

SWANSON: I think if you are a COO, the job should be in the two-to-four-year range. I would say that if at the end of four years you don't have the top job, you ought to be looking elsewhere, if your desire is to be a CEO. On the other hand, being effective in the number two position is about more than not staying in the job too long; it's also very important to have something you can sink your teeth into. I told Dan, for example, that I wanted to create a customer focus within the company. As a result, I had something from the start that I could concentrate on, that I could take with me across the company to our team—my own message. When I went out to see our people, I talked about performance, relationships, and solutions—what we consider the three pillars of a customer-focused company. Dan had his messages and I had mine, and they complemented each other. The point is, you need to have your own stamp on something. You need to be measured.

AUTHORS: As an internal hire to the CEO role, your ability to get started is different than that of someone who parachutes in. What are the advantages there?

SWANSON: The hardest thing for someone parachuting in is to understand the culture. What are the hot buttons? What makes the place and the people tick? If you want to feel the pulse of this company, just watch what happens when we start talking in employee town halls about the importance of saving lives. We're in the business of saving lives—whether we provide systems and services to our men and women in uniform, air traffic management systems that guide passengers to safety, or business and special mission aircraft. Saving lives is an important mission—our people feel that and respond to that—and anyone who is leading Raytheon also needs to understand that about our culture. The internally developed CEO is brought up with that feeling. He or she understands from day one that employees want to engage their jobs that way, to wrap around this important mission. It can take an outsider a longer time to identify the message that will resonate. The same is true in relationships with customers if you come in from a different industry.

4

THE SEARCH FOR A COO

I start with the premise that the function of leadership is to produce more leaders, not more followers.
Ralph Nader

Once an understanding of how the key competencies might be identified has been established, the next challenge concerns how candidates are identified and vetted. If a decision for an external search is made, executive search consultants are typically retained. To begin to understand the characteristics associated with successful performance as COO, we interviewed John Thompson and Joie Gregor, both vice chairmen with Heidrick and Struggles. Each has extensive experience in conducting senior executive searches and, from this experience, an understanding of the core competencies necessary for someone to effectively perform as COO.

INTERVIEW WITH JOHN THOMPSON, VICE CHAIRMAN, HEIDRICK AND STRUGGLES

AUTHORS: Let's start by looking at the COO role from the recruiter's point of view. When you are engaged to find a COO, what exactly is it that you look for?

THOMPSON: Frequently, strong candidates have demonstrated a love for operations. They see and are energized by the challenge of either fixing something that is broken or making changes that help organizations become more successful. The best candidates are individuals who have shown the ability to address the business's problems by quickly adapting and to productively partnering with the CEO. What you want to avoid is a candidate who seems focused on the question of how quickly they might become CEO. If there is a conflict of expectations or a demonstrated inability to quickly form productive work relationships with others, or an expressed or implied view that the job is no more than a stepping stone, our radar goes up on high again because that can be a warning of problems down the road.

AUTHORS: So operational excellence and willingness to roll up their sleeves and get into the detail sounds like something that is very important. What else comes to mind?

THOMPSON: I would say a significant tolerance for both complexity and ambiguity is important because these roles tend to be somewhat situational around the individual. If a person needs everything written down and locked down in order to be comfortable with the job, the COO job is likely not for them. In many cases, you are sharing a role with someone else, and the way each individual contributes evolves. The way the role has evolved at Dell Inc.—between Michael Dell and first Mort Topfer and then Kevin Rollins—is a good example.

AUTHORS: Does the COO have to be a strong strategist as well?

THOMPSON: Many people view the CEO role as being more about strategy and the future and the COO role as being more about today's operations. However, a COO who is not capable of strategic thinking is a disaster. You have to be able to think strategically in order to implement. That is a very damning remark, by the way. When people label someone as a "good operator," it is about as stigmatizing for an executive as saying a person uses drugs. It creates a stigma, accurate or not, that people remember. Regardless of whether there is any truth to it, if you say somebody doesn't have any strategy skills they are going to have a difficult time succeeding as a COO, and even more so trying to move into the CEO position.

AUTHORS: Decision-making ability must be a critical competency for COO candidates. Can you comment on that?

THOMPSON: Yes. Decision-making ability is critical for anyone in a management position—but it is particularly critical for a COO because of the nature of the decisions typically made. Making a deep cut in staff, selling a division, closing down a business, closing down a product line, no one feels good about making those decisions unless they are truly sadistic. On the other hand, people with high levels of managerial competence can find pride in knowing that they have done the right thing. It doesn't mean it is not difficult.

COO candidates have shown they can make the tough decisions. They know they need to make them and they have the ability to reflect, after the fact, on the decision and know they did the right thing even though it was very difficult to do.

AUTHORS: What else would you say is a critical COO competency?

THOMPSON: These people tend not to have high needs for public, outside exposure. They tend not to be people who seek out having their picture on a cover, or whatever, because they don't enjoy it or just view it as a distraction. They don't want to take time to even do it. If a person has high needs for ego satisfaction and stroking, etc., then you are also looking at a risk factor. No matter how competent they are to do the core of the job, if they have an ego that needs attention then the wheels may come off the vehicle at some point. Also, they tend not to rely so much on position clout and power as they do on their own influence skills. They find a way to be comfortable being viewed as the implementer of someone else's vision. Finally, the best candidates love to coach and mentor people. Mort did that with Kevin Rollins. He enjoyed that because when Kevin started reporting to Mort, Kevin had never been a general manager. His background was in consulting.

AUTHORS: Do COOs make great CEOs?

THOMPSON: There is nothing to keep them from becoming one. Where there has been a very good mentoring relationship and there has been some planned transition by the CEO, such as "I want you to be with me on my analyst calls," "I want you to go with me to get the external experience," "I want you to be at board meetings," etc., then the COO is well positioned to be successful in the CEO role. That said, there are some COOs who are truly operational in their competency profile and they are not well suited to become the CEO. Such is the true inside person—they are outstanding in terms of the value they can add inside the company, but they would be a disaster as the chief executive.

AUTHORS: Where do you find great COOs? Just considering several notable COOs—Ray Lane, Mort Topfer, and Bill Nuti, for example—these guys came from very different backgrounds. One was a consultant, another was a senior executive at Cisco Systems, and the other spent twenty-five years at Motorola. Where does someone best develop the right set of competencies to be an effective president or COO?

THOMPSON: Both Kevin and Ray came from consulting [one from Bain, one from Booz Allen and Hamilton]. They probably gravitated toward working on operational types of projects, strategy projects—in other words, "What is wrong with this? Why is this not getting done?" or "This organization design does not fit with the strategy of the company," or "We have a customer loyalty problem, we have customers defecting from their brand; how do we fix that?" In Mort's case, he was just ending a twenty-five-year career with Motorola and I recruited him to Dell to simply be Michael's mentor. Soon after he assumed the number two position—it was then called vice chairman. At the time of his recruit, Bill Nuti was one of the highest-potential executives at Cisco Systems. He was clearly going to be ready to be a CEO on a time horizon that was incompatible with John Chambers's likely exit. I recruited him into Symbol Technologies as the CEO-elect. He obviously has continued to grow and now serves as CEO at NCR. As you can see, there is no one defined place where you can go to find a COO. Many times the search is designed around the situational needs of the company, along with their fit with the company culture and complementarities of skills with the CEO.

AUTHORS: Does the COO inevitably want the CEO role?

THOMPSON: Potentially. There are some people that I think are natural second bananas, to use a slang term, and they don't have any real interest in being number one. For example, after Ray left, Jeff Henley for practical purposes has served as the chief operating officer for Larry at Oracle, and Jeff didn't want to be the CEO. He had no interest at all and served this role in a de facto manner under the vice chairman title. I think the board poked him on it numerous times. He just had no interest whatsoever. That wasn't what he wanted to do. He tends to be a private person; he didn't want the personal public exposure you have when you are CEO of a public company, especially a large one. When people want to know what you did over the weekend, where you go on vacation, what kind of car you drive, what kind of house you have, and offer that "Gee, isn't that over the top? Why do you have that kind of car?" or "What kind of charities do you support?" or "What political party do you support?" it gets to be a bit much. He tends to be a very private person comparatively to what CEOs have to put up with because it is like being a rock star or in entertainment. If you don't like to see fans or you don't like to sign autographs, sooner or later that is going to be a problem—that is part of the territory in the CEO role. It doesn't mean you have to stay two hours and sign autographs, but it does mean if you are just a total jerk all of sudden the fans and the press, the Hollywood press, the entertainment press, the board press are going to be all over you because you are seen as a poor sport. You don't really understand what the position responsibilities are and costs are. Personally you complain about how you can't go out to Denny's anymore.

Some companies use the chief operating officer role as a developmental spot, not just as a place to hand something off. A company that has done a great job at that is Intel. Paul Otellini served as COO and just became the next CEO. And Andy Grove did the same thing. IBM has used that model

---

WHAT TO LOOK FOR IN A COO CANDIDATE

1. *Does the person have a strong interest in operations?*

2. *Does the person have credibility in the industry?*

3. *Does the individual show a strong results orientation?*

4. *Is there evidence that the individual is a capable decision maker?*

5. *Is there evidence that the individual will be quick to learn about and adapt to the organization, especially in terms of the company culture?*

6. *Is there reason to believe the CEO and this candidate will be able to quickly develop a very close and trusting working relationship?*

7. *Does the person have strong interpersonal skills?*

8. *Does the person have a clear understanding of the four corners of the COO position, as it currently exists?*

9. *Does the person have an accurate understanding of whether or when this role leads to the CEO position?*

10. *Is there reason to believe this individual will be able to check his or her ego at the door?*

with Sam Palmisano, becoming COO before assuming the CEO position, a role they hadn't used for a long time. GE hasn't used it, but since they are so large they have these large operating roles anyway, and essentially in many of their businesses they have Fortune-sized P&L's that are run by many number twos. What they did do during the transition of Jack Welch to Jeffrey Immelt was have Jeffrey shadow Jack for an eight-month period in order to get the full enterprise view of the company. This extended period of learning is great and is always available for internal candidates, if the company is doing its succession planning properly.

INTERVIEW WITH JOIE GREGOR, VICE CHAIRMAN AND MANAGING PARTNER, HEIDRICK AND STRUGGLES

AUTHORS: Tell us what you view as the key skills to effectively serve as a COO.

GREGOR: You have to be an enormously quick study. When you walk into a room, you must be able to identify the issues and understand who are the key players. It is essential that you have an ability to build trust, confidence, and gain the respect of those around you almost immediately. You must also be able to quickly get the core issues, e.g., Why are we missing our revenue targets? Why are expenses too high? Is the current business plan attainable? You have to drive by analysis, not emotion, as well as an ability to size up just about any business model that comes in front of you. You must also be able to move from the day-to-day operating details to the strategic level seamlessly.

AUTHORS: Why does a company need a COO?

GREGOR: There are actually several reasons. Oftentimes it is pace—market demands. When the complexities of operating issues are broad and deep, a CEO just may not have the bandwidth to tackle everything. He or she may need a partner with strong operating skills who can assist in the execution of the business plans to ensure success. In the early days of Oracle, the company was moving at such a fast pace that its infrastructure was not keeping up with the demands of its customers. The ability of its employees to deliver on their commitments was in question. In that case, the founder and CEO, Larry Ellison, brought in Ray Lane, who turned out to be an excellent complement to Ellison. The company needed discipline in order to scale, and Ray was able to bring that on board given his earlier experiences at IBM, EDS, and Booz Allen. It was a great partnership for many years.

AUTHORS: There had been no discipline in their process?

GREGOR: Not really. Oracle was growing at such a fast pace, the company was out of control. Everything was about driving sales. They had hired an excellent group of very aggressive sales representatives with a less-than-sophisticated services and support team behind them. It was absolutely the right thing to do—bring in an executive who had seen size, scope, and scale in order to develop an infrastructure capable of satisfying their customer set and continue driving growth.

Another model is simply to develop or train future leaders. For example, Intel recently moved their president and COO, Paul Otellini, into the CEO seat. This, of course, was a planned succession move as Craig Barrett assumed the chairman role. For several years, Paul was able to broaden his skills in the president and COO role.

AUTHORS: In Raytheon's case, Dan Burnham created the president role to broaden Bill Swanson.

GREGOR: Burnham was considering his own succession plan and was initially not sure if he had an internal successor. After carefully assessing his executive team, he created a new role entitled president, responsible for Raytheon's government and defense operations, and placed Bill Swanson into that position. Bill had run a number of business units at Raytheon and this was similar to a finishing school. It gave the company an ability to see Bill in action handling a much broader scope of responsibilities, both with the board, the external community, and their customers. He was forced, if you will, to take an enterprisewide view and see how things were interconnected at the highest level. He also was able to spend more time with Dan and the board talking and thinking about the business. Dan was able to successfully retire after about a year, and Bill has been a wonderful success story. This is a great example of a proactive succession planning process where an executive was given the appropriate time to enhance his skill set and prepare himself for the top job, similar to that of Otellini at Intel.

AUTHORS: Are there cases where a COO is the wrong move?

GREGOR: Without question. If the board is trying to support a weak CEO, it just will not work. We have seen this a number of times, particularly in smaller companies where the investors are afraid to pull the plug on the existing CEO, particularly if they are preparing for an IPO in the not-too-distant future. It is difficult, given the perception that it may send to their customers or potential shareholders. It does not pay to support a weak CEO with a strong COO. Most importantly, you are not going to get an A player (COO) to support someone who is failing. In most cases, you are much better off changing out the CEO versus adding a COO. Why delay the inevitable?

AUTHORS: Are there any other key COO competencies?

GREGOR: A COO has to have a really interesting repertoire of operating and leadership skills, almost chameleonlike, with the ability to subordinate their ego to that of the CEO. Undoubtedly, they need great financial and execution skills, but also good instincts and the courage to make tough decisions that are fact-based. Certainly, they must be confident and comfortable as a person and as a leader.

AUTHORS: It also sounds as though CEOs must be comfortable in their own skin so that they can have somebody who is strong beside them.

GREGOR: No question about it. They must be mature and relaxed about the relationship; they cannot second-guess their operating partner, but still be able to give him or her input as necessary. Both must be good communicators, able to define their roles, eliminating mixed messages and confusion.

AUTHORS: Trust is so critical between the two.

GREGOR: My guess is that Michael Dell, in his worst hour, would not question whether Kevin Rollins has done his homework. I doubt if that would happen. I also doubt if Larry Bossidy would have questioned Fred Poses. It does not mean that Michael and Kevin, or Fred and Larry, would not have disagreements, or differences of opinions. The answer is clearly yes. In both cases, their working relationship would have to be on the basis of trust, and certainly emotional maturity, in order for them to succeed.

SUMMARY

In this chapter, interviews with two search consultants who have been regularly involved in searches for top-level executives reinforce some of the themes previously discussed, as well as offering several new insights into the COO role. Thompson and Gregor both talk about the importance of (1) being comfortable outside the spotlight, (2) being results-oriented, (3) establishing a trusting relationship with the CEO, and (4) being skilled interpersonally so that relationships with other members of top management are artfully developed. Beyond those comments, these consultants note that a danger COOs need to be aware of is being labeled as merely a good operator. The label is seen as building a ceiling that could prevent the COO from ever having the chance to serve as CEO. This points to a dilemma that COOs must consider when planning their career: By doing a great job as a number two, are they, at least for some, creating the impression that they cannot go any further?

At the same time, Thompson and Gregor both point out that not all COOs have the right stuff to serve as CEO. Though the CEO and COO positions require some similar strengths (e.g., strong communication skills, ability to establish rapport with a range of people), the context in which the work takes place differs. The CEO operates under what can be a harsh spotlight of attention; the COO is many times one step removed from that spotlight. Of course, this positioning presents a Catch-22 of sorts; the ability to operate away from external scrutiny affords protection while also making it difficult to "show what you can do." A further difference executives shared with us is that it is difficult to anticipate how different decision making is when there is not a check or balance above you. Both CEOs and COOs have to make tough decisions; for the CEO there is no higher authority from which to seek affirmation or support. Even in those instances where the COO has the ability to handle these aspects of the CEO job, the ability to practice (with the public, with the board, and so on) is going to exist only to the degree that the CEO creates opportunities. So, even though the COO role is an avenue to prepare someone to take on the responsibilities of the chief executive, it does so only if the CEO is deliberate about and supportive of this effort.

A CONVERSATION WITH CRAIG WEATHERUP

DIRECTOR, STARBUCKS
FORMERLY CHAIRMAN AND CEO, PEPSI BOTTLING GROUP

Craig Weatherup has been a director of Starbucks since February 1999. He was chairman and chief executive officer of the Pepsi Bottling Group from November 1998 until January 2003. From July 1996 until October 1998, he was the chairman and CEO of Pepsi-Cola. He is also a member of the board of directors of the Pepsi Bottling Group and serves on the board of directors of Federated Department Stores (http://www.forbes.com/finance/mktguideapps/personinfo/FromPersonIdPersonTearsheet.jhtml?passedPersonId=224003).

AUTHORS: In your words, what are the key skills, experiences, and competencies for someone in a COO position?

WEATHERUP: I think the key requirement for that individual is to have a very broad set of competencies—ranging from sales to operations to marketing, R&D, international, legal, financial, you name it. Depth is wonderful, but from my experience through PepsiCo or Starbucks or Federated—the floor for any COO's success (and CEO for that matter) is a good, broad, experiential set of competencies. I think in terms of the other pieces of success, the CEO and the COO must make sure that there is absolutely clarity in their leadership and managerial roles and how the work is shared. I think the COO needs to be comfortable that he or she is able to act as the CEO from day one, because there have been in my experience CEO dimensions that you need to pick up right away. You need to be comfortable and capable of picking those pieces up. Obviously, the CEO and COO can't second-guess each other. If one of you screws up, you have to stand back to back. I think underneath that is, if there is not a dimension of trust—and I would go further than trust to even friendship—I think it will work, but it works pretty poorly and I have seen it many, many, many times. I mean deep down, you have to trust each other and you have to like each other. If you don't like each other, or don't trust each other, it may work, kind of, but it will be at a 50 percent level at best.

AUTHORS: As an individual transitions from the number two to the number one, are there any gaps in experience that you would expect to see emerge?

WEATHERUP: There are two things: one, as a COO, they have not learned, or haven't gotten comfortable with the fact that they are now on the point all the time—twenty-four, seven. When the PR person calls up because somebody threatened to put cyanide in one our bottles or something, you get the call—it is always that. I went to my guys and said, "If you really want to lead something, there are no time outs." Someone who has been COO should know that, but until they have to work that way, they don't understand it. I think the other thing that makes people move successfully from COO to CEO is the ability to constantly be articulating the vision, the strategy, the critical initiatives—driving the company's culture, and so on. Some people find that easier to do than others. Again, as the CEO, you really need to be the one to do that.

AUTHORS: Is it better to have the COO with a different set of skills and experiences in comparison to the CEO, or similar?

WEATHERUP: I have seen it work both ways. If I looked at Starbucks, I have been a friend of Howard Shultz a long time, long before I joined the board. Howard and I are more good friends than anything else. He is chairman today, so let's assume he is the number one guy; a guy named Orin Smith is the CEO, so it is not quite the COO in terms of title, but they are clearly number one and number two. Orin was the chief operating officer before, and they very much have complementary skills, and they are very different people. Howard was the founder, the visionary, the Michael Dell kind of thing. Orin was more the operating executive, very much so—came out of the CFO job. They complemented each other very, very well.

At Pepsi, I would say with Roger [Enrico] and myself, for example, our skills are far more similar, but we have very different personalities. Skillwise, we are similar—we both spent some time internationally, both were marketers way back when, both spend most of our careers as GM types, and both of us have this propensity to really dig in and know the business. On the other hand, Roger was a very charismatic kind of guy and I do my thing a little differently than he does. I think it worked well because we had complementary personalities. I personally would prefer to have fundamental skills that are somewhat complementary and then have some differences in skills, some differences in experiences, some differences in personalities to round it out.

Not to carry this too far, but sharing some "dark alley" experiences at Pepsi-Co helped the two of us learn to work well together. Roger was running the snack business in Japan, which was losing money. I was running the beverage business in Japan—which was also losing money. Both businesses were tiny and both were getting killed. It is our private joke that when Don Kendall [co-founder of PepsiCo] came to town, we would compare notes ahead of time so he couldn't fire both of us. Having some common difficult experiences helps a lot later on when you are trying to have a shorthand conversation about "Losing a share here, we have this problem there, or this challenge here."

AUTHORS: How long can someone serve as COO before appearing plateaued?

WEATHERUP: That is a great question. I do think there is. . . . There is maybe one or two in ten where it works for someone to be COO for life. It is right for the person, the company, and the CEO. I would truly think that eight out of ten times there is shelf life, but the really good COO is every day more a CEO, and therefore at some point, most likely, that person will either conclude, "I'm good at this, I'm ready to be the CEO at this company or someplace else" or "I'm not good at this, and I'm going to go do something else," and it may be another COO job but it may be a totally different job too. I think most of the time you either fail or succeed, and you succeed as becoming a CEO or you fail as the COO-in-waiting and you go do something else.

I'd say it is no more than probably three to five years before it is "up or out" for most COOs. At the same time, I'm sure there are some instances where somebody is the COO for a long time. Take Don Keough at Coke. Don was the COO a long time—he retired as COO. He was a very high-profile and successful executive, but the number two for a long time.

AUTHORS: Do you have advice for a new COO?

WEATHERUP: I think first you make sure you sit down and clarify the roles and clarify the decision-making responsibilities. Getting the mechanics of the job straight are important so nobody trips you or the CEO. Obviously one of my questions as a COO is, Do I think the CEO is competent? I have been in situations where, in my junior executive life, I thought my boss wasn't competent.

Basically, at the end of the day if this individual doesn't have the character, if they don't see leadership as a privilege and care about followership and so on, then it isn't going to work. It is not going to work for you, and it is probably not going to work for the organization either, and it is certainly not going to work for you as the COO. I think you need to sort though this competency side of this, the mechanics and so on, but you also need to sit down and really spend the time on, Does this individual the CEO have the kind of character that you want to partner with, the values? And if not, you shouldn't go there. You won't be successful and you will hate it.

A CONVERSATION WITH DEL YOCAM

CONSULTANT

FORMERLY COO, TEKTRONIX AND APPLE COMPUTER

Del Yocam is an independent consultant. He was chairman of the board and chief executive officer of Borland Software from December 1996 until his retirement in April 1999. Prior to joining Borland, he was an independent consultant from November 1994 through November 1996. From September 1992 until November 1994 he served as president, chief operating officer, and a director of Tektronix—a provider of test measurement and monitoring solutions for mobile network operators and equipment manufacturers. Previously, he ran Apple Computer's Asia Pacific business and served as Apple's first COO.

AUTHORS: From your perspective, what are the key competency skills and experiences to be successful as a COO?

YOCAM: The role is a very complex role. At Apple, I grew up within the ranks from middle management to top management. I started as director of materials, became vice president of manufacturing, vice president of operations, executive vice president and general manager of the Apple II Group, where I was really running my own company within a larger organization. Once Steve

[Jobs] was ousted, I was given the additional responsibilities of the Macintosh, became executive vice president of product operations and then chief operating officer. There is nothing that can replace experience.

When you have that kind of track record, you have an advantage over anyone brought in from the outside, because nothing can replace those years of experience within the company. I had made my name internally, and the employees knew what I was all about. And whereas I had immediate buy-in from the employee base, John Sculley, who came to Apple from outside the industry, didn't. Even after ten years as Apple's CEO, I wonder if John ever experienced the kind of support that I had from Apple employees.

Once I was offered the job of COO, it became necessary for me to make sure that we understood the lines of demarcation—in other words, as COO, what became my responsibilities versus John's as CEO. John and I were able to work that out early on, while I was EVP product operations. His role was the strategic leader of the company and the direction of the company, the strategic plan, the external relations—with shareholders, industry pundits, analysts, etc.—was his responsibility. My role was the operations leader of the company, and I ran the company on a day-by-day, month-by-month, quarter-by-quarter basis. In many ways I was Mr. Inside and John was Mr. Outside. You have to have these defined responsibilities decided up front to make sure that you are able to do your job. One more thing I would add is that you have to make sure that the communication lines are always open between you and the CEO so that there are no surprises down the road, either way.

To do your job, you have to know how to lead people. The best way to learn that is by being thrown into a situation where you are forced to learn how to survive and then manage, then lead. For me that happened at the Ford Motor Company, right out of college, where they had a long-term management-training program. To weed people out, they threw you out onto the manufacturing floor, with the UAW, to see if you could not only survive but manage and lead. My initial assignment was the setting and unloading of railcars (boxcars) at 4:30 A.M. supervising men who could care less if I survived let alone succeed. With them, I learned how to survive, I learned how to manage and finally learned how to lead. Over the next four years, I held increasing levels of responsibility in all functions within the automotive assembly plant from my initially being a line foreman to section supervisor and finally held managerial positions. After two years at Ford Division Headquarters, I decided that my future in the automotive industry looked too structured for me and turned to high-tech for excitement and the unknown.

I guess, going back to characteristics for one final point, I think one of my strong suits was confident decision making. I really believe in the decision-making process of defining the problem, gathering information, open discussions about the information, determining alternative courses of actions, selecting the best alternative, implementation, and follow-up. I always knew that selecting the best alternative was my decision unless I delegated it to a subordinate. But even then, it remained my responsibility.

AUTHORS: The CEO has to be comfortable in the role, and you need to communicate and work together collaboratively as a team to get the organization to a certain place.

YOCAM: Exactly. In fact, I wish that John and I had worked more collaboratively as a team. What happened at Apple was that John was writing his book and he was not there an awful lot of the time during the two years that I ran the company. It was almost like one day after John's book was published and he had done all the interview tours, he began looking internally and realized how much power this guy had, this number two guy. If there was any paranoia that began to step in, it was that realization, and thus, if you recall or look it up, you'll see that he decided to make four presidents of Apple Computer, Inc., a title he had promised me. When I couldn't convince him how ridiculous that was, because I had been running the company for over two years, I gave him my notice that on my tenth year anniversary I would leave. I then took over responsibility for Apple Pacific in my last year at Apple because I believed it wouldn't succeed if I didn't handle it personally; I had been the one to separate it from international and knew it was a great growth opportunity for us. The rest of the story is history. It's interesting that John—and he would tell you this himself—came back three different times to see if I would come back and run the company or some part of the company (e.g., an Apple Education Company). After I had made that decision to leave, I wanted to have the opportunity for the number one job; I didn't want to spend any more time at Apple because with John I had no idea of his future plans and how long he wanted to stay at Apple.

In relating this part of the story, I believe that had the two of us spent more time together the outcome could have been different. In one way, I enjoyed the freedom that I had; but in the long run, his writing the book worked against me and really against the company. I think it would have been better if we had worked together collaboratively as a team to get the organization to a certain place during those years.

AUTHORS: When you think back when you were in that role, what things kept you up at night as COO?

YOCAM: I lived it day and night. I had enough information coming into my computer at home or telephone overnight that when I woke up in the morning, even before I went to the bathroom, I could begin to learn how we had done the previous day from a sales and manufacturing standpoint. The job of COO is an around-the-clock job. Whether a new product introduction, a sales forecast, or a manufacturing response, it was my responsibility to make sure that operations ran as planned. The COO has to be very close to the business day in and day out. You have to live that business, and ultimately that's where power comes from—from your ability to make more right decisions than wrong decisions in running the company.

AUTHORS: In terms of an organizational design, how did Sculley and you arrange reporting relationships?

YOCAM: John had the CFO, general counsel, Business Development, and me reporting directly to him. I was responsible for Advanced Technology, Product Development, Worldwide Manufacturing Operations, Worldwide Sales, Marketing and Distribution, and Information Systems and Technology.

AUTHORS: You mentioned leaving Apple for that chance to be the CEO of a company—when you got that opportunity, what gaps did you find in your preparation?

YOCAM: Because of my having been COO at Apple and Tektronix, I was pretty well prepared. The missing piece is often the strategy piece. However, I am a strong believer that you cannot separate strategy from operations in a general business sense. I had to ensure that John Sculley at Apple and subsequently Jerry Meyer at Tektronix understood that there is strategy in all aspects of the operations of a company. Operations strategy is separate from the CEO responsibility of vision, long-term strategic direction, and the strategic plan of the company. But the COO, in running the company, has to incorporate both strategy and operations in the development of the annual plan (supporting the strategic plan), meeting quarterly expectations and results, and in planning, organizing, staffing, directing, and controlling all aspects of the operations. Operations management is an art as well as a science and is taught in most all of our business schools.

AUTHORS: In terms of advice for people who currently are president or COO, do you have any advice for them as they move into that role, the CEO role?

YOCAM: I think you need to get into the heads of your board of directors. You need to have a dialogue with each director and understand where they have been, where they are currently, and where they are willing to go with the particular company that you are looking at to become CEO. I wish I had done that with Borland. As CEO, you are going to want to put your own imprint on the company, and you may want to take it places that the current board of directors have not even thought of and may not in fact endorse. In hindsight, I wish I had taken the time to spend with each of the Borland directors prior to accepting the position of CEO, to understand their individual business philosophy and where they wanted to see the company go in the future—the company's direction. Ask the questions: Do you want evolutionary change or revolutionary change? How fast? Over what period of time? How much stamina do each of you have for change? Do you want a short-term or long-term strategy? You cannot ask too many questions. And more importantly, listen carefully to the answers.

AUTHORS: How about advice for someone considering a number two position?

YOCAM: You have to have the experience of increasing management responsibilities in various functions within the industry. One of the human resource activities that Apple became famous for was allowing employees to move from one discipline to another. It is not a common practice even today in many industries. I was very fortunate to have been accepted on the Ford Motor Company's Management Training Program in the 1960s that allowed me to experience all aspects of automobile assembly management. And Apple was very innovative in the 1980s in high-tech, allowing cross-discipline movement of employees within the company. Breadth is important. Situational leadership is important. There are many ways to accomplish whatever the objectives are of the company. But unless you have experienced an increasing level of management within various functions over the years, you will not have the background necessary to successfully run a company as COO. Of course, there are always exceptions, but as a general rule you need to prepare yourself for your future, and one of the ways is by getting cross-functional experience.

One of the biggest mistakes a COO can make is getting into too much of the detail. With the right preparation, the right experience, you will have developed gut-level instincts that take over and thus not require you to go too deep within any one function. Once you have tested your direct reports, back off and let them do their respective jobs. If you go into too much detail in any one function, you may miss the overarching problem that you are trying to solve or the opportunity that you are after or the competitive advantage that allows your company to win.

And stay above the political fray. Sort out in your own mind what is right and wrong. Be willing to make all decisions; but delegate as much as you are comfortable doing at any point in time. Remember, you are responsible for running the company, and that means the management of the company. And management can be defined as planning, organizing, staffing, directing, and controlling. Do your job and manage. If you develop and meet each annual plan to support your CEO's strategic plan, you will not have to concern yourself about longevity in the role of COO. And it can be a very exciting and fulfilling role.

A CONVERSATION WITH ROBERT HERBOLD

HERBOLD GROUP
FORMERLY COO, MICROSOFT

Bob Herbold served as the COO of Microsoft from 1994 until 2001, a period of time during which the company experienced a dramatic increase in both revenue and profits. Prior to joining Microsoft, he spent twenty-six years at Procter & Gamble. He recently launched the Herbold Group, which consults with CEOs on strategy and profitability issues. His service at Microsoft offers a good example of how the COO role functions when it is quite clear to all that the incumbent is *not* an heir apparent to the CEO position.

AUTHORS: From your experience at Microsoft and P&G, can you give us a sense of the key competencies required to be successful in the COO role?

HERBOLD: Let me start out by indicating that I don't think there is a single thing called "chief operating officer." I think there are a number ways to assemble responsibilities in a way that creates a job that can easily carry that title. If you look across industries, you see is a whole lot of different uses of that title. So it is important to note at the outset that we are not talking about some rigid, specific definition of a job. As a result, the key competencies are not universal.

If you consider my COO role at Microsoft, my job was to handle the business issues of the company while Steve Ballmer ran sales and I worked for Bill [Gates]. . . . Steve and I both worked for Bill; Bill ran the product group, Steve ran sales, and my job was to handle all the business issues so as to keep them out of Bill's hair. That is a different role than say Kevin Rollins had for Michael Dell at Dell Computer. Kevin has evolved from a COO kind of role to one of actually sharing leadership of the company with Michael. Today, the two of them run the company and they kind of parcel out what they each do well, and it matters not what titles you put on these guys. So the role is quite varied, company to company.

That said, at Microsoft the finance organization and the CFO worked for me, the corporate marketing people worked for me, and I watched over the marketing activities that were going on in those divisions so that they were consistent with what we would want to do as a total company. I managed the manufacturing arm and distribution arm of the company, as well as human resources and public relations. The competencies required to do those things are (A) a lot of common sense, and (B) a lot of experience in dealing with a variety of business problems that come at you from many angles, so you want someone with a broad set of experiences, not necessarily deep in a particular area but deep enough so that they really can contribute as well as keep things together. So I came to the job with a ton of marketing experience, with a ton of IT experience (IT also reported to me).

AUTHORS: **Is there an ideal way to structure the content of the COO role?**

HERBOLD: Sometimes it is just a function of the people involved. The chemistry between the individuals has to be very good. So, one of the things that I had to do with Bill Gates and Steve Ballmer is that we all had to know what we were going to do so that we didn't fall all over one another and surprise one another. So constantly working towards that is very important. I have seen examples— one company in particular comes to mind—where they had a COO in a role similar to the one I had. There was always tension between the CEO and the COO because, frankly, the CEO had certain ideas on how some of these areas would be run and the COO wouldn't come to grips with that. And so those shared expectations as to "what are you responsible for" and "what am I responsible for" are so fundamental to making the leadership work—without it, there is clearly trouble ahead. Right now at Microsoft, with Steve being the CEO and Bill running the product groups, they have to be very careful because Bill is the software architect and knows where he wants to take the products and he is a great mind in that area. Steve needs to work very closely to keep up with Bill, and they need to thrash that out and make sure it continues to be thrashed out on an ongoing basis.

AUTHORS: **You could conceptualize the COO role as interesting because there is a sense that you are simultaneously leading and following at the same time. How do you define the decision-making structure so everyone knows who owns what?**

HERBOLD: You are onto something really important that often leads to disaster if it is not nailed down. To me, this is a key issue, and the way it gets worked out is the individuals, through trial and error, as well as through discussions, figure out who is going to be doing what and who needs to check with who on key decisions. There are some instances where confidence will be developed and the individual goes off and just does things. There will be other instances where the decision is sensitive enough that both parties, or three parties, want to be involved. Those things need to be discussed as to how we are going to work these things out on an ongoing basis very early in the relationship.

AUTHORS: It sounds like the relationship—building trust—and then having a very open and honest way of communicating with each other—is critical.

HERBOLD: That is very true. If you look at Kevin Rollins and Michael Dell, they worked close enough for a long enough time that they know exactly what each is going to be doing. Bill and I developed this relationship. On crucial things, where there was going to be big impact, we naturally worked the detail in terms of what we were going to do and then I just went off and did it. That is what he hired me to do, to isolate the important ones, come to a quick agreement within fifteen minutes as to what we want the final picture to look like, and go out over the next several months and do it.

AUTHORS: At Microsoft, you were the outsider brought in to break all the glass, to make the changes that needed to be made. Bill functioned more as a keeper of the culture, coming in behind that transformation and bringing everything together.

HERBOLD: That's exactly right. There is no doubt he is the spiritual leader of the company and continues to be today. It is a clever move on Microsoft's part. Bring somebody in from the outside, develop this triad leadership model, agree what is going to be done, have the COO in place to make the changes, and allow Bill—and Steve—to continue to focus on the vision for the future.

Another thing that is important is in terms of long-term expectations held by the COO. When I went to the company, I had no interest in being the CEO. My job was to have fun solving all these problems. I signed a four-year contract with the complete intention to retire at its end. Now, it ended up lasting a whole lot longer than that.

AUTHORS: What advice do you have for a COO who, like yourself, is coming in from outside a company?

HERBOLD: They should make sure that they are clear in their mind as to what they want to have happen, what kinds of things they want to do, and what sort of resources will be required to get the job done. Then they need to review that with the chairman, the CEO, or whoever—depending on the structure of the company—and hear what they each want to do and they each expect from the COO. At a very, very early stage, get those things pounded out because people notice it immediately when people are stepping on one another. There has been a lot written in regard to when I decided to retire and we are on this go-ahead path with Steve evolving to the CEO; getting the relationship squared away between Steve and Bill took a little time, and there have been stories written about that. They got it squared away. It is very important for that to happen quickly.

AUTHORS: What was the biggest surprise when you took the job at Microsoft?

HERBOLD: The speed of the industry and consequently the need for a lot more informal decision making. Procter & Gamble and Microsoft are very similar in that they hire really good people. And they both strive to have their products preferred by their customers versus the competition's; they have good focus on getting the products right. The difference is the speed of the industry. From a technical standpoint, it is harder to get a little wine stain out of a white shirt than it is to double the capacity of a microprocessor, and so you get this industry that is just screaming along—this is primarily during the 1990s and the early 2000s; it is not screaming so much today—so you have to move. You have to make decisions very quickly, very informally, and I wasn't exposed to so much at P&G. Within a couple of weeks, you soon begin to say, "OK, this is how things have to be and why they have to be that way."

AUTHORS: From your own experience, is there anything missing in the COO role in regard to preparing someone to be the CEO?

HERBOLD: I think the big gap is that people have to understand that the buck stops with the CEO. Namely, the CEO has to make some fairly gutsy decisions at times with incomplete data. And it is possible to do the COO job and not have any experience doing that. So, that is an important element. Another thing that is important is, Suppose you were a COO that only had business unit experience, where you made those tough decisions about the product, for example, but you have no experience in terms of how to operate the place. You'd get killed. Both kinds of roles are relative to the COO: important, gutsy product decisions and important efficiencies and ways to actually run the company from an IT, HR standpoint. Those are important, and you see a lot of CEOs that only have one side of that experience.

A CONVERSATION WITH JIM DONALD

PRESIDENT AND CEO, STARBUCKS

James L. "Jim" Donald joined Starbucks Coffee in October 2002 as president, North America. In this position, he was responsible for the overall management, business development, and operations of Starbucks in all North American markets. He was promoted to president and chief executive officer effective March 31, 2005. Prior to joining Starbucks, he served in a variety of key executive positions with Wal-Mart, Safeway, and Pathmark Stores, where he served as chairman, president, and CEO.

AUTHORS: You left a CEO position at one firm to take a position with a "lesser" title at Starbucks. Some might say there is an inherent risk in taking a step backward like that. What was it like to transition from the role of CEO at Pathmark to your initial position at Starbucks?

DONALD: As I made the decision to say yes, all my CEO buddies out there said, "You made the worst mistake in your life; you never give up a title." And so, when we made the announcement that Orin retired and I was taking over, they all e-mailed me back—you would think they would say "congratulations," but they said, "You got lucky on this one."

AUTHORS: In a sense, you have a number two role now, with Howard as a very involved chairman. What can you say to people who are going into a number two role? What do they really think about before accepting that sort of position?

DONALD: What they have to remember if they want eventually to become a CEO is that what got them to the role of a president and COO won't necessarily earn them a CEO role. Though they did something to earn a president and COO title, things that one needs to do to prove that they could run a business, like making numbers, are not the same things you need to do to be CEO. Once you are in the COO role, you have to make the numbers, but then you have to broaden your network of things you do. You need to work with the board, work with the CEO, and work to lead others to be successful. And you have to understand that if you don't have a great number one to learn from, you are not going to have the latitude and longitude to do what it takes to become a number one yourself one day.

AUTHORS: When you came to Starbucks as the number two, Orin was the CEO. What did you do—coming in as an outsider—to build the relationship?

DONALD: You have to take it a step back even further. First of all, I came in to take the place of Howard Behar—the most loved and trusted soul in this company. And don't forget, it was "H2O"—that was the slogan, two Howards and one Orin. So the first step was to convince everybody that I was not going to ruin what Howard Behar built. Knowing that in two years I would be taking over for Orin, I hit the ground running. I had to prove that you could run the business from the Howard Behar standpoint, but then I had to develop an army of support across the world of people that were midmanagement and senior management. I had to prove that I had the capability, the understanding, and the processing abilities of an Orin Smith. So right away, knowing that these two guys were just legends in this company, I had to prove myself in a way that fit with respect to the culture. Starbucks is different than other companies; if the culture doesn't accept you it will spit you out in a heartbeat. I tell new people that all the time. While I was trying to grasp the role of this new business, I was also trying to placate everybody's fears, that it was going to be OK, that I am not a bad guy.

AUTHORS: You make a great point: Coming from the outside, without the benefit of positive history with the company, you have to build credibility and trust quickly.

DONALD: Not only that, but it was up to me to do it. It was not up to the people to accept me; it is up to me to earn acceptance. That is no different from when I came in as the chairman and CEO of Pathmark. In order to turn that company around, I couldn't walk in like I was the chairman and CEO. I spent the first four weeks in the field, practically around the clock, probably talking to over five thousand of the twenty-five thousand employees, convincing them that I was here for them. Because of that kind of start for me, those people gave me the support I needed when I had to start making tough decisions.

AUTHORS: Can you talk a little bit about the top-level relationship, specifically with Orin and Howard, and how you defined who did what without tripping over each other?

DONALD: I call this a great example of succession planning. I spent years under Orin and Howard, but as I look back it was the absolute best thing I could have done because Orin and Howard gave me a free runway. Orin was more of an administrator, financial type and I am kind of the operator, merchant type—we complemented each other in terms of skills. Orin, bless his heart—I just saw him yesterday and gave him another hug for it—he let me do what I needed to do. I would check with him, and with Howard too, but I ran Starbucks like I had been there for ten years and knew what the heck I was doing. Orin allowed me to do it.

I don't know why exactly, but the three of us just clicked from day one. As I would do things, I would give them a heads up and they would either push back or say "Fine, go ahead." They would caution me about this or that but they really let me run things as I saw fit. Orin gave me air cover to travel the globe in terms of immersing myself into the business. As a number two you need to be both a good lieutenant and a good general. As a good lieutenant, I stay in touch, then with Howard and Orin and now with Howard—whether they want me to or not! I do that to this day with Howard. I will call Howard when he is in Dallas and I will say, "What's up?" He'll say, "What do you mean?" I'll follow with, "Nothing, just checking in." It will drive him crazy, but he knows that I'll keep him informed—I will do my part to make sure we are always joined at the hip.

AUTHORS: Would you say that another action that can help gain buy-in to a new COO is for the person to begin by assessing people internally for promotions as opposed to bringing people from the outside?

DONALD: Exactly, and to create no surprises in the short run. The very first week I got here, I froze hiring; I wanted to get the lay of the land. Everyone said "Here he goes; this guy is in the supermarket industry, cutting cost." My old nickname came back as just a cost cutter, but I told Orin and Howard, "I just want to see what I have before I make any moves." Long story short, I didn't hire anybody from the outside, but I broadened the responsibilities of the people who were in here and promoted them. I asked everybody for their resume going back three jobs ago. I spent weeks reviewing these to see if they could handle what I had in mind or if I could shift them here or move them there. It was really kind of neat. The loyalty that I gained by not bringing anybody in and giving them these new roles, it still exists today.

AUTHORS: **When you came in as the president, what was the relationship with some of Howard's previous direct reports? How did the whole configuration of relationships to Howard work, and with Orin as well?**

DONALD: It was up to me to earn their respect first and foremost, and then it was up to me to make the decision whether they would be my direct reports or not. I had to earn their respect first before I could even make that first move. There have been some changes in some of those particular positions. It took a long time and involved partners here that quite frankly the job outgrew.

AUTHORS: **One of the things that often happens is that people who were the direct reports try to find a back door to the CEO, or in this case to Howard as well. How do you prevent that from happening? Is it a concern?**

DONALD: I encourage it. I say if there is something that I am doing that you don't particularly like and you want to go talk to Howard, go after it. By and large, by allowing that, it rarely happens. First of all, when I got here, people were saying "Aw, Howard is going to swoop in; Howard is going to do this; Howard is going to do that." After about four or five weeks, I just called a meeting and said, "Let me tell you guys something: You don't know how fortunate we are to have a Howard Schultz at this company. All companies need a Howard Schultz. The founders and entrepreneurs contain a passionate enthusiasm that nobody else has because they saw from store one to store ten thousand." I said, "My goal is to leverage all that passion and enthusiasm and make him a continual part of this." If a guy had an ego, he couldn't do what I did coming in with Orin and Howard. He couldn't do, like you said, two in a box. People with egos, the other CEOs that have these egos, won't allow themselves to operate in this manner. It is a sad thing to say, but it is true.

AUTHORS: **You are one of many to say that you have to check your ego at the door and that you have to work hard to stay aligned with the number one.**

DONALD: Who in their right mind wouldn't listen to what Howard would say with a comment or a thought? This is what he does. The day-to-day stuff, he doesn't want to do it, nor would I want him to. I couldn't have done what he has done nor have that creative side of my brain thinking about the things that he does.

AUTHORS: **The way the number two role is designed seems to be company-specific as to whether it is succession, turnaround, expansion, growth, or whatever it happens to be. How do companies think about measuring that role in terms of performance?**

DONALD: We don't have a COO now; I have four presidents reporting to me. In all likelihood, because of our plans for growth in three to five years I am going to have to have a COO. I have eleven direct reports now and that might move to thirteen—that is too much. I continue to consolidate and go global, versus having silos. I would measure a COO not necessarily off the performance measure that got him or her in that position but their potential to take on more. Ideally, I think the system would include board involvement and would consider to an extent duties that CEOs normally do versus COOs.

AUTHORS: **You have moved back into the CEO role. From your experiences in each position, what is really missing in the COO job in terms of preparation to become a CEO? Were there big surprises when you transitioned into the top job?**

DONALD: Let me answer that in two parts. From day one when I walked in, Orin had already started pushing some of his direct reports to me as I was running North America. When Orin and I made the announcement in October, all of his direct reports came over to me, even though he was the CEO until the end of March. I had six months of having all of these direct reports reporting to me, and so the last two or three months I was basically running it. There was never that big transition. Now when I went in from a senior vice president, general manager of Safeway to the chairman and CEO of Pathmark, I was very naïve about the role of the CEO, and it was good thing. I used all my operator skills for the first six months to one year, which normally a CEO wouldn't do, by going into places and riding with truck drivers to really assess the problem. At the end of that year I said, "Wow, we have bigger problems than I had thought." I would have never have seen those problems before. I went out and did a COO role as the chairman and CEO—it was a good thing, I wouldn't recommend it, but I wouldn't say "Don't do it any other way" because you have to find out what the heck is wrong with your business, as we did at Pathmark.

AUTHORS: We talked to Ed Zander, who was the number two at Sun and is now CEO of Motorola. He had a COO when he came into Motorola, and he moved that guy out. He said, "For the next three to five years, I have to learn the business, figure out what is wrong with it, and then if I need a COO, I will do it."

DONALD: I think if I would have had a COO I might have done the same thing. I can't have anybody between my eleven direct reports and me now. First of all, I am very accessible to them and to take that away in the middle of growing from ten thousand to twenty thousand stores I think wouldn't be the smartest thing to do.

And I think another thing, this kind of goes with checking ego in at the door. I have been doing a lot of talking to universities and some not-for-profit groups, and the first thing out of my mouth is, "I wake up every day and say this is really impossible; how in the world can you be running Starbucks?" It is as humbling as it can get. It is really realizing that no matter what you are the CEO of, you have to understand that you are one fortunate son of a gun to be doing it.

AUTHORS: It is one of the world's brands and a great company. Talk a little bit now about two in a box with Howard. How do you make that work?

DONALD: I think you have to be compatible first of all. But second of all, I think that it is incumbent upon me to make it work, not Howard. It is obviously Howard's company, but how I look at this is that I have certain strengths and I have certain needs; Howard clearly does as well. I don't go to Howard with any of the day-to-day stuff, such as how we are going to spend $600 million in capital. That is stuff I have been doing all my life. I go to Howard and say, "I'm thinking about this idea; can you give me your thoughts?" Or "What about this platform that has this new-age beverage, what do you think about this?" Howard has such a gut-feeling instinct for that stuff that it is like having a mentor right next door. It works in that way. Howard doesn't want to approve capital.

He doesn't want to know the ROI that these particular stores exceeded. He doesn't want to do that anymore; he did that. It really works well.

AUTHORS: **He is guru, strategic advisor, founder, and mentor.**

DONALD: But I will also tell him when I am speaking to my direct reports—and this is the same thing I am talking about—I will say, "You mind sticking your nose in for fifteen minutes?" and he will. It is using Howard to leverage stuff. Let's say I am really making a point, and Howard comes to this point, everybody is thinking, "Why is Howard here? It must really be important." I just kind of use it in that manner and it is good that way.

AUTHORS: **Is there a natural life span to serving in a number two role, or can it go on forever?**

DONALD: I think in a company like Starbucks that is global, a company that is going to have thirty thousand stores in fifty countries, it is a full-time job forever, once we get to that point. The reason is because, number one, growth is a great thing, not for shareholders but for having career opportunities for partners. It is unbelievable when you can retain a partner by saying, "What other company would you want to go to? Why wouldn't you come here when I tell you we are going to triple the size of this thing and there are businesses you can run?" The COO role is a natural one to be able to career-path senior executives and have that step in there. It gives them one more box to aspire to, and it is good to have the position in there. I need it, though, just simply because as this entity gets big my demands will be too. I never thought having ten thousand stores would be an easy thing, but to get to thirty thousand stores with all of the different constituencies out there, my demands are going to be pulled away from the day-to-day activities and I need somebody there. I will say that COO will be my replacement.

AUTHORS: **This brings us right back to your earlier comments about succession planning.**

DONALD: And they need to know that. He or she needs to know that when I make a COO, I am down to three to five years left. I am a big believer in succession planning. I am a big believer in going too deep in every position. You lose some and then you have to replace them back in, but you just never know.

I just want to make a point, and I say this to all the up and comers: I have two presidents now; one runs international, one runs U.S. They do 90 percent of our business in profits/sales. In my midyear with them, I told them that I love what they are doing, I love their skill sets, but that is not enough if they want to be the CEO. "These are some of the things I want you to start doing to be a CEO. First of all, you have no interaction with the board; I want you to start picking that up. Secondly, you guys don't interact with your peers, the rest of my team, and you need to do that with finance, with legal, and you need to keep them in touch, but you also need to learn from them. And third, both of you need to talk to each other, international needs to run U.S. and U.S. is going to have to spend some time international; the earlier you start it now, the less time you will have to do. Keep doing what you are doing, but you have to do more if you want to take the next step."

A CONVERSATION WITH SHANTANU NARAYEN

PRESIDENT AND COO, ADOBE SYSTEMS

Shantanu Narayen is president and chief operating officer of Adobe Systems. In this role, he is responsible for the company's day-to-day global operations and for developing the vision for Adobe's diverse product lines. Together with CEO Bruce Chizen, Narayen has grown Adobe's business to nearly $2 billion in annual revenues. Since joining Adobe in 1998, Narayen has held a mix of key product research and development positions, including vice president and general manager of Adobe's engineering technology group, senior vice president of worldwide product development, and executive vice president of worldwide products. Before coming to Adobe, Narayen co-founded Pictra, an early entrant in the digital photo sharing business. He previously served as director of desktop and collaboration products at Silicon Graphics and held various senior management positions at Apple Computer (http://www.adobe.com/aboutadobe/pressroom/executivebios/shantanunarayen.html).

AUTHORS: From what you have learned at Adobe, what do you see as the key skills and competencies required to be successful in the COO role?

NARAYEN: The most critical skill for a COO is the ability to fully understand the company's strategy and then translate it into executable plans. Bridging the strategy and the operational execution is the unique demand placed on this role. As part of that execution, a COO has to build the organization and create a structure that enables solid results. A COO also requires adaptability, because in the role, by definition, you are complementing or rounding out either the CEO's or the top management team's skill set. The last element is having an operational bent—there are lots of spreadsheets and process details that need to be managed and understood. In the end, however, if you can't conceptualize the strategic objectives or help drive them into an executable plan, then you aren't going to succeed.

AUTHORS: What factors are necessary to ensure a good CEO-COO relationship?

NARAYEN: To make it work, you must be really clear about expectations—what you are doing and what the other person is doing, where you spend your time, when you check in and when you don't, and so on. After a while it becomes second nature and you don't think about it, but initially taking a little time to understand these expectations is really critical. Overcommunicating on a wide variety of things is also important. The last key thing is complementary skills. If you both like doing the same things or are good at the same things, there is a lot more second-guessing and less appreciation than if you bring different skills to the table. Those are the key elements of a successful CEO-COO relationship for me.

AUTHORS: When you talk about communicating, how do you make sure there is enough opportunity for it?

NARAYEN: Bruce (Chizen) and I probably have more one-on-ones with each other than I have with my staff, and I would suspect it is the same for him. Informal communication is important, too. Having an office next to each other, having an open door, frequently inviting each other into meetings ad hoc because something is interesting . . . that builds a relationship. For example, this week I drove in with Bruce and we got some time in the car. We also periodically travel together. That is one of the best bonding opportunities, because you are sharing an experience—whether it is talking with customers, or visiting employee sites, or dealing with the press. It provides chances to work together outside the office. You come back with a much better appreciation for what employees and customers are doing and a shared perspective.

I suspect that one of the attributes for success is a close working relationship prior to being publicly anointed number two. I think I would have been disadvantaged if I was hired from the outside at this level. That would have made my job ten times harder than being inside the company and demonstrating that I could have more impact and take on more authority. I would bet the most successful one-two pairs are at firms where it has grown from inside, as opposed to one or the other coming from outside the company.

AUTHORS: How do people feel who used to report directly to the CEO and now report to you? Is there tension there, and are they looking for the back door to the CEO?

NARAYEN: I think as people get more senior, the distance from the top is more important than the distance from the bottom. There is no question that people like a personal relationship with the CEO. Bruce and I want these executives to know they are respected members of the team, and we agree on which decisions each of us will make. You have to keep the door open to the entire team—it's up to Bruce and me to ensure that we are always on the same page. That is a delicate balance for both of us.

AUTHORS: Several of our interviews have surfaced the issue of ego as something that is destructive in the CEO-COO relationship. Can you comment on that?

NARAYEN: It boils down to who the two individuals are and whether they have a common strategic direction that they want to take the company. At the end of the day, if the strategy of the company is not shared between the CEO and COO it just won't work. Ego is certainly one of the defining criteria for success or lack of success in that partnership.

The other common scenario is that the CEO is not ready to have a second-in-command, to give up some of the leadership. That creates a whole basket of problems for the number two. Bruce is very, very good at reaching out to me and saying, "Are you having fun, are you enjoying yourself, is there anything I can do to help?" And it's genuine. Shortly after my promotion, there was a social event in Bruce's family and he invited a handful of us from Adobe. His father and his brother approached me and said they were really pleased about my new position. It was clear to me that Bruce had told them how excited he was about my new role. That really means a lot.

AUTHORS: As you transition from your EVP role to the COO role, any surprises so far?

NARAYEN: For me, one of the biggest surprises has been my own drive and desire to be successful in my new role. The pressure I have put on myself has increased dramatically from my previous role, and my wife has commented that I seem a little stressed and I'm working even harder than I used to. But I'm also having a very good time—it's a great learning experience and has been very rewarding.

The other surprise has been my sense of urgency around setting the organization up for success. I have an opportunity and obligation to build a scalable organization and get the right people in place for the company's strategic direction. That is the challenge: How do you build the right team that is empowered for success, and do it while the bus is still on the freeway?

A CONVERSATION WITH BILL NUTI

CEO, NCR

FORMERLY CEO AND COO, SYMBOL TECHNOLOGIES

William Nuti has recently been selected to be president and chief executive officer of NCR. At the time of our interview, he was president and CEO of Symbol Technologies. Nuti joined Symbol as president and chief operating officer in August 2002 after having served for more than ten years with Cisco Systems. During his time at Cisco, he held a variety of positions, culminating with an appointment as the senior vice president of the U.S. Theater Operations and Worldwide Service Provider Operations. In that role, he managed Cisco's field operations, systems engineering, professional services, and marketing for the global service provider arena as well as their U.S. sales divisions, including enterprise, service provider, and commercial business.

AUTHORS: **You were recruited to Symbol to be the number two. What did you expect you would face in the role?**

NUTI: If you are brought in as a COO, your job is essentially to drive operational excellence throughout the company. You have to be detail-oriented; you have to like to roll up your sleeves and get into the details with your teams. You have to have very little to no ego if you are going to be the number two because the CEO is largely going to be the face of the company externally and you are going to be the face of the company internally. When you think about being recruited as the number two, you either have one of two goals: one, you want to be a CEO and hence this is a great step forward for you; or two, you really enjoy being the process engineering leader for a CEO—being a number two, helping that CEO to establish himself or herself and the company as a leader in the industry. Hence, quite frankly, you go forward with a lot of confident humility, all the time knowing that you are not going to be someone who is going to receive a lot of the accolades when things go well. And probably you will receive a lot of the blame when things don't go so well.

AUTHORS: **How difficult was it coming in from outside the company? How did you go about establishing productive work relationships with the CEO and the rest of top management?**

NUTI: The relationship side of the equation is an interesting one because the first thing you need to do is establish credibility. When working to establish credibility with the team, you must know that there are going to be those people on the team who have close relationships with the CEO, and you cannot ignore that. And frankly, you cannot try to get in the way of that. You have to expose the team to the CEO as much and as often as they would like to be exposed but at the same time make sure they understand their role in achieving the stated goals and objectives. You need to work very hard at building relationships because, in the COO role, it is all about the respect and the trust of the people that work for you and their key people who really make it happen in the trenches. That will feature prominently in your ability to achieve the corporation's goals.

The other key relationship, of course, is with the CEO. If you understand the vision and the goals of your CEO, you have worked out with your CEO the internal plan to achieve those goals, and you both are in sync, and you have a CEO who understands that he or she needs to allow you to do your job, then you have what you need to be successful. You then meet regularly and partner very closely with your CEO, providing regular updates as to your progress.

AUTHORS: It sounds as though one strategy would be to not try to do too much too quickly, but instead focus on finding some quick wins to get some positive momentum.

NUTI: Clearly that is the case. Here at Symbol, it was easy for me to do because the low-hanging fruit was all over the place. But if you think about it, it is not just the short-term wins. The way you gain credibility with a staff who does not know you, who did not work for you, and now there is a layer between you and the person they once worked for, is to listen. And listen very clearly and have courage, the courage to listen over periods of time and not be ready to jump in with a solution on day one because you think you know better or because the place you came from did it a certain way. You have to be an extremely good listener and not let your past experience become a barrier to future success. This is where lots of new COOs who come from the outside fail. Most feel as though the knowledge they learned in their past company is transportable to the new company—and sometimes it is not. Don't forget what you learned; just don't always be thinking about a smart answer when you should be listening and learning.

AUTHORS: People in new roles seem to feel as if there is an action imperative—they want to do too much too quickly.

NUTI: Correct. The first thing you need to do is build a one-hundred-day plan that forces you to get to know the organization—both its strengths and weaknesses. After you have spent time getting to know your customers and partners, your people, the organization structure, internal processes, current strategy and the company's past . . . you'll be in a far better position to set in place a focused set of objectives that are aligned to the needs of the company. I strongly recommend the strategy of "focus and overwhelm" when you do decide to implement change. Take the top three things that require attention and communicate them to the organization: why they are important, what value the focus will bring, and the measures and metrics you are going to use to track progress and speed of execution.

AUTHORS: How important are complementary skill sets between the CEO and COO to making the organization successful?

NUTI: What worked extremely well at Symbol was I was Mr. Inside and he was Mr. Outside. That didn't mean Rich [Richard Bravman] didn't dip his nose in. We had a phrase here with Rich. I said I was fine with "nose in," but "fingers out." I was fine with him asking questions, I was fine with him dipping his nose in and looking into things and getting a sense of things, but I wanted him to keep his fingers out. I was buried in a turnaround effort. But in this particular case, I like the concept of inside and outside. Certainly there were times when I represented the company externally, and certainly there were times when I wanted Rich to be inside using his subject matter expertise—in his case, engineering—and exercising them in areas where I knew I didn't have as strong of a skill set. We consciously discussed those things, talked about them, and made sure we executed in a symbiotic way so we were not running over each other and confusing the organization.

AUTHORS: To continue in that vein, it sounds like you spent effort up front establishing clarity around the entire relationship. Over time, that must require a great deal of course correction along the way.

NUTI: Constant. Mind-numbing. And very transparent. It has to be, otherwise you will run into a strategic disagreement or an operational disagreement with your CEO. Your team will feel it, and that is destructive to the chemistry of the senior team, and it is destructive to the ability of your company to move at the pace you need in this industry to win. Absolutely.

AUTHORS: It seems like there are a lot of number twos in technology. Almost every tech company either runs two in a box like Gates and Ballmer or Dell and Rollins, or has a very defined number-two position. Any insight into why?

NUTI: Yes, the reason why that has been the case predominantly over the last ten years is because growth in tech has outgrown just about any industry on the planet. That growth has been the number-one driver of the creation of the number-two position—along with the change management that underpins growth inside of a company to stay on top of your game. The second reason has been competition. Tech is a hotly competitive industry, unlike many other industries. I'm not suggesting other industries are not competitive. What I am suggesting is if you look at capital formation over the last ten or fifteen years, no one needs to go further than the venture capital community to see where capital formation was happening. It was happening in the tech center. You are dealing not only with traditional competition and markets but new competitors that grow up each and every day. So the competitive dynamic was also a big contributor to the two-in-a-box process that took place because a CEO really has to be focused also on the external as well as the internal factors in a company. The bandwidth of the CEO, given the two key factors of growth and competition, did not allow them to run the company at a pace and at a speed that was consistent with their ability to be competitive long-term.

AUTHORS: What advice would you offer someone thinking about taking on a COO job?

NUTI: Know why you want to be the number two. Absolutely understand and be very clear with your CEO what your goals are. That means, if you are coming into the COO role and your goal is to eventually be the CEO, that has to be understood before you join the company. Because if you have a CEO who is going to stick around for a decade or more, you may not be able to reach your goal at that company. But your CEO has to realize that after five years you may be leaving the company because you really want a CEO job. If your goal is to come in and be a really solid number two to support that CEO and you don't want to do the external side of the job and you really just want to be a great COO, that has to be clearly understood as well. That means your tenure in that position may be longer than the life span of most COOs, and it may mean that you and your CEO are going to need to understand what the succession plan is, going forward for the next CEO. Those are critical things to discuss.

AUTHORS: Is there a life span for the COO who wants to be the number one?

NUTI: Absolutely. First of all, it depends upon the company you join. At Symbol, given everything that needed to be done in a turnaround effort, to be a

COO here for more than a few years would have been difficult at best, because every year was like a dog year, or seven years. We were working a multitude of things at a pace that is not representative of most healthy companies. If you are going into another company where the operational underpinnings of the company are good, then you are looking to go from good to great. Let's face it, at Symbol we went from awful to good. To go from good to great is a different set of circumstances. I would believe that the average life span of a very good COO would be four to five years in a good-to-great scenario.

AUTHORS: **Thinking about the transition from number two to number one, what was missing, or what were the biggest surprises becoming number one?**

NUTI: The biggest surprise for me as CEO is that you really cannot divorce strategy and execution. They are one and the same. You have to own strategy and you have to own execution.

The second is the amount of time it takes to manage and participate on your board of directors. It is hard work and it takes a lot of time. It is an enormous time-and-bandwidth drain, and it is frustrating if in fact you have come from a COO role where you are into the game every day. You are into the mix. You love it. You roll up your sleeves, you are coming in, you are talking to all the leaders of your businesses, you are doing operational reviews, functional reviews day in and day out. And you realize that now, a good portion of your day is board recruitment, board management, board preparation as well as meeting and dealing with financial analysts, the press, etc. The external side of the job becomes much more so a bandwidth drain, and you have to have a very strong operational infrastructure to be able to withstand that. You miss the chance to be hands-on with the business.

5

ATTRACTING AND MANAGING

A COO

Some people are better at being number twos.
Silvio Dante, The Sopranos

Identification, recruitment, assimilation, and management of an effective chief operating officer are challenging and critically important processes. As we have discussed, the COO role is a highly complex leadership position, for several reasons. Search consultants are quick to note that it is one of the most difficult assignments they face, because of the complexity of the role and the concomitant broad range of necessary knowledge, skills, and abilities (KSAs) that must reside with viable candidates. Making an external hire to the COO position is by nature high-risk. Not only is it the senior operational role in the organization, bound by financial, operating, and other organizational performance requirements, but also it is characterized by nuance and highly reliant on a set of complex relationships with the chief executive officer, the board, the leadership team, the broader organization, and myriad external constituencies. Echoed throughout our interviews was another source of complexity: that effective CEO-COO relationships are characterized by many emergent qualities. They are hard to anticipate systematically, which would then permit them to easily influence the selection process. Finally, understanding the true nature of the motivation for hiring a COO is of great importance. What it takes to get it right with respect to COO selection is likely to vary according to whether the overriding goal of the hiring is firm-focused, CEO-focused, or COO-focused. In each case, the organization must grapple to understand the configuration of personal characteristics, competencies, and experiences that would predict the success of an individual in the role of COO.

Beyond understanding the business motivation for the COO role and its consequences for selection, decision makers also need to consider the personal fit among the COO, the CEO, and other members of top management. A theme repeated in our interviews concerns the essential role that a deep trust between CEO and COO plays in making the relationship a success. COO success is largely dependent on the relationship with the CEO; thus the interpersonal connection between the two executives must be such that it fosters this deep trust and an intense commitment to sharing responsibilities, accountability, and control. Because trust develops over time, COO candidates who are already familiar with the CEO may be more attractive. In the absence of such familiarity, all parties involved would be well advised to plan on starting the relationship off on the right foot by personally investing in building the relationship well before the COO comes on board. Additionally, respondents regularly raised the issue of role definition for the COO; of particular importance is an understanding, shared by the CEO and the COO, of where one's responsibility, authority, and decision making end and the other's begins. Each of these issues—trust and role definition—is by its nature idiosyncratic to the CEO-COO pair. As such, they are particularly daunting dimensions in regard to maximizing the fit between a COO and an opportunity.

WHERE TO BEGIN?

The process of selecting a COO should begin with three major considerations in mind. Though they seem like obvious requirements, they are not always addressed, and even where they are their complexity is rarely fully appreciated:

1. Is the business rationale behind—and therefore are the goals expected to be achieved through—creation of the position sound as well as consistently understood by the board and the top management team?

2. Is the CEO fully prepared to share (which is typically heard by CEOs as "give up") power and support the COO's authority as legitimate?

3. Is the CEO prepared to commit to a significant investment of his or her own time and energy in the success of the number two, both before and after hiring?

Just as the firm seeking a COO should carefully reflect on these questions, so too should the individual considering such a position. If these criteria have not been met, an incoming COO is certainly at a disadvantage with regard to chances for success.

Question One:
What Is the Business Case?

What is the business case behind creating the COO role? Has it been effectively communicated throughout the company?

The CEO-COO configuration is far more likely to be accepted if it is conceived with good intentions. We have identified three broad motivations for creating the role: firm-focused, CEO-focused, and COO-focused. The greatest legitimacy to the claim that a COO role is necessary exists in the first case, where there is a clear business imperative behind creation of the role. Whether the firm needs to create an inside-outside team at the top in order to cope with a turbulent environment, industry demands, and daily operations, or to bring leadership to a strategic initiative of great importance, the business case for the position is easily made.

There are also instances where CEO-focused motivations for creating a COO role are easily understood as legitimate. Such is the case, for example, when the position adds particular skills to the management team that the CEO does not possess, or when the role makes needed mentorship available to a developing CEO. That said, there are instances where CEOs have decided to bring COOs on board so that they can experiment with retirement. Additionally, we heard stories of CEOs creating a COO role so as to have a place to unload those aspects of the CEO role they find less enjoyable. The expectations of a lighter load or a desire to concentrate only on areas of personal interest are not a good rationale and are unlikely to be accepted if recognized as such by a board, savvy members of an organization, or external constituents.

Of course, there are also COO-focused motivations for creating the position that easily pass the test as appropriate. For example, a succession-planning strategy often benefits from bringing in a number two who can acclimate over a period of time before taking over as the chief executive.

Finally, we identified the decision to create a COO role as a method of retaining executive talent. Clearly, the appropriateness of this strategy—to "park" an executive in a place that makes it difficult for him or her to be dislodged by other firms—may have its place but is certainly not always defendable. In fact, efforts to save an executive by offering the COO title may in fact be viewed with such suspicion by other members of top management as to hasten their exit from the company.

Question Two:
Is the CEO Prepared to Share Power and Support the COO's Authority?

For a COO to be successful, the CEO must be prepared to share power. Practically, this requires that the two partners create, communicate, and continuously pursue a vision for the organization. The CEO has to be ready to give up some control over critical aspects of operations. Structurally, the CEO will likely be required to divert to the COO other top executives who were formerly direct reports. Obviously, CEOs have to be vigilant about not facilitating efforts by these individuals to circumvent the COO, because to do so essentially erodes the COO's authority.

The reality is that in many ways bringing in a COO creates a situation that is more—not less—demanding on the CEO in terms of effort, hours, and often the strain on personal humility. However, the benefits to the CEO and the firm, if the COO role has been deliberately conceived and is subsequently carefully executed, can be tremendous.

Question Three:
Is the CEO Ready to Invest in the Success of the COO?

The CEO must be prepared to work diligently to properly bring the COO on board. Our conversations with CEOs who have been through this process unequivocally stress the importance of checking ego at the door and just as consistently describe how difficult this is for most C-level executives to do successfully. It is likely necessary for the CEO and the COO candidate to spend a great deal of time together before offers are extended to ensure value alignment and the ability to build a trusting bond. To build trust, one must take risks—in the context that risk is proportional to the autonomy offered to the COO. The same risk is mitigated by the amount of trust the COO has earned. So the CEO

THE ROLE OF THE CEO IN EFFECTIVELY IMPLEMENTING THE COO POSITION

Prior to the Search

- *Has the CEO accurately self-assessed his or her own strengths and weaknesses so as to understand how a COO might be complementary in regard to competencies?*
- *Has the CEO identified and communicated a clear case for creation of the role?*
- *Has the CEO given considerable thought to the four corners of the COO position?*

During the Search

- *Has the CEO built an effective relationship with the search firm so that the consultant has a detailed understanding of the critical selection criteria for the COO?*
- *Has the CEO invested sufficient time with each candidate to build a foundation for mutual trust?*
- *Has the CEO worked with candidates to evolve the four corners of the position and to make sure there is mutual understanding of the boundaries of the position?*

After the Search

- *Has the CEO continued to make the necessary investment of time to establish effective communication and trust with the COO?*
- *Has the CEO worked with other members of top management to clearly demarcate where the COO's responsibilities begin and end?*
- *Has the CEO properly managed current and former direct reports so that a back door can't be used to erode the COO's authority?*

During the COO's Tenure

- *Does there continue to be a shared understanding throughout the COO's tenure of the likelihood of the position serving as a path to the CEO job?*
- *Has the necessary seamlessness in communication and decision making been created and nurtured?*
- *Does the CEO regularly expose the COO to the board in a way that highlights good work and capabilities?*

needs to be in a position where he or she is willing to face such risk. After the announcement, the CEO will be busier than ever helping the new COO come on board and establish authority, all the while preventing sabotage of the new arrangement on the part of any disgruntled executives.

THE SEARCH FOR A COO

The search for a COO likely involves a number of parties: the board, the CEO, a search firm, other members of top management, and some number of hopeful COO candidates. The board must review and validate the decision to create a COO in the first place and then must make certain that the CEO is pursuing the best candidate—for example, someone who will work within the company's values and culture, someone who complements the capabilities of the CEO, and not just someone who will handle the tasks the CEO finds unattractive. To add value, the search consultant must manage these parties to ensure that all are engaged in the process and fully aware of their responsibilities. The search consultant must ask a lot of tough questions and challenge the thinking and rationale of the client throughout the process. As is the case with a business acquisition, the more work you do up front in the due diligence phase, the easier it is to integrate on the back end. Without a true understanding of the commitment required from each participant in the process, the search will not be successful—and instead potentially result in the sort of CEO-COO configuration that leads to poor company performance.

The Search from the Perspective of the CEO

The CEO's personal investment in selecting a COO begins with the decision to create the position. It continues with active engagement in the search process. Time is required to meet with finalist candidates to assess interpersonal chemistry, values alignment, and cultural fit with the top management team and the larger organization. The requirements on the CEO's time, however, have just begun once a candidate is identified and the courting begins. The posthire requirements of bringing on a number two are enormous. This process ideally starts many weeks before the COO physically arrives on the job. In some cases, it bridges the end of the formal interview process and may even begin before there is a signed offer letter. For example, Ken Freeman had no less than seven meetings with CEO Surya N. Mohapatra before he came aboard as the number two at Quest Diagnostics.[1] For internal appointments to the COO position, the time available for on-boarding is more easily extended; the convenience of the candidate being located inside the company should not lull management into shortchanging the process in any way. Michael Dell and Kevin Rollins spent a great deal of time together before Rollins officially became the company's number two (he joined in 1996 and oversaw various functions and operations before becoming president in 2001).

A successful situation, as at Dell, Intel, or Quest Diagnostics, does not occur by chance. It requires a tremendous amount of interaction between the CEO and COO candidate before the CEO-COO configuration is implemented. During the search process, the chief executive must spend a great deal of time with the number two. This is because once a candidate is selected the two need to *quickly* forge a very strong, trusting relationship; there will be no time for concern over ego gratification or for suspicions of a hidden agenda or musing about ulterior motives. The CEO and COO candidate should know whether they will be able to communicate openly and honestly with each other and whether they will be able to spend long hours together without growing tired of one another. Our interviews suggest that this is not a relationship where you can dislike each other and still perform your duties optimally.

As the search progresses, the CEO must be mindful of a number of issues that can affect successful assimilation of a newly hired COO. For example, once on board, formal and informal interaction is critical. The methods and manner in which the two executives interact send an important message to other members of the organization. Seemingly simple gestures such as setting up the COO's office proximate to the CEO's can itself be a powerful communication. Physically co-locating makes it clear that the CEO is relying heavily on the COO's input and expertise. In addition, this arrangement facilitates communication, which is absolutely critical throughout the life of the CEO-COO configuration.

The CEO should be sure to allow time for sharing and continuously reinforcing his or her strategy and vision for the company with the COO. Post-hire, it is absolutely critical that the CEO and COO be aligned with regard to vision and strategy. There should be no confusion here; if there is, it will certainly spread throughout the organization. Eventually, the COO will be required to selflessly implement the CEO's vision and strategy as if it were his or her own. Thus it is important that the CEO ensure up front that the COO truly buys into the CEO's strategy and vision as if it was his or her own and is 100 percent committed to its successful implementation. Once the number two is on board, the CEO and COO need to operate with an identical understanding and deep command of the details of the vision and strategy so that, whether the CEO is speaking to the press or the COO is speaking to plant employees, there is complete consistency. Any gap will be perceived as lack of focus, lack of agreement on strategy, or a rift between the two executives. Strategic alignment is a critical element to a successful CEO-COO partnership. It must be constantly monitored because if divergence occurs it can lead to passive-aggressive behavior and undermining tactics, which can be fatal to a company and to one or both executives.

Similarly, during the search process the CEO should discover the COO candidates' philosophies on the COO role. Once on board, the CEO and the new COO must invest considerable time meticulously defining roles and decision-making protocol for the entire top-management team. "It is absolutely critical that the number one and number two be crystal clear on who is responsible for what," says Wendell Weeks, Corning's president and COO. Like strategy and vision, if a COO candidate's philosophy regarding execution of the COO role differs materially from that of the CEO, it is likely that these issues will not be resolved.

In addition to investing a great deal of time and energy on communication, vision, and strategy alignment, the CEO must prepare to subordinate his or her own ego to set the stage for a successful CEO-COO configuration. This is often difficult for chief executives. They must share information readily with the number two, whereas in the past they may have been the only one with complete information about the business. If the CEO does not make this change, the COO is operating with incomplete information, and the perception emerges that the number two may not be fully trustworthy (or that the CEO is hiding something).

Whereas sharing information is difficult for some CEOs, the thought of sharing power may be even more daunting. Since COOs are presumably brought in for real, strategic reasons, it is hard to imagine a CEO-COO scenario in which the CEO will retain the same level of decision-making authority and control as he or she had before the number two arrived. Once a COO is brought on board, the roles must be clearly defined and the decision-making responsibilities and protocols well sorted out. Yet, once faced with this prospect, most chief executives equate sharing power with abdicating it. Further, CEOs may become perplexed when they see that sharing power has not brought a corresponding reduction in workload. Seeing no fair trade-off, they may resist relinquishing power and try to retain decision-making authority (or, worse, publicly overrule the COO). In either instance, such behavior on the part of the CEO can be a fatal blow to the relationship and may ultimately threaten company performance.

The fact that information and power sharing are such difficult adjustments for most chief executives reinforces the importance of CEO efforts, during the search process, to fully engage on the business and personal levels with the candidate. A CEO must share all information with the incoming COO and thus must be completely comfortable with the executive, and quickly establish a high level of trust with him or her. Also, the CEO who is considering adding a number two should interact regularly with the search consultant, revisiting the implications of sharing information and power and constantly testing whether the CEO is prepared to commit to the success of a new COO.

The CEO should prepare to share information and authority; he or she should also facilitate speedy establishment of the COO as a capable leader in the company. One of the most effective ways of doing this is to identify early wins for the COO. The CEO should choose visible opportunities that will have some impact, work to ensure the COO's success, and then celebrate the successes publicly. Not only does the outcome give the COO credibility but the process of setting up the quick win has the effect of (1) building the COO's trust of the CEO, (2) facilitating alignment between the two, and (3) developing a CEO's confidence in the number two. It makes a great deal of sense for the CEO and COO to map out a plan to secure these wins during the on-boarding process. Failing to do so increases the chance of an early derailment for the COO.

A CEO should also be mindful of the life span of the COO role. Though they acknowledged that the occasional exception likely existed, our respondents converged on an effective COO life span of three to four years. This figure is a critical consideration for CEOs, and it is—to some degree—a function of the initial motivation for creation of the COO role. If a business has a critical need that requires intensive operational focus from a number two, the life span of the role could be much different than if the CEO and board are seeking a succession candidate to learn a highly complex firm or nuanced industry. In the first case, the life span might be defined by the time it takes to bring the crisis under control—perhaps twenty-four to thirty-six months. In the second case, the span could stretch over five or more years. Such was the case with Kevin Sharer at Amgen, who was in the number two role for seven years before ascending to the top spot. If the CEO and COO do not have a discussion about the expected tasks and tenure, there could be an unhappy parting of ways. Larry Ellison, for example, hired Ray Lane primarily to address the immediate issues centered on the ailing U.S. operations. Though Lane was quite successful in stabilizing that situation, as his role became less crisis-oriented it also became less well defined. Eventually Ellison began withholding information from his number two. According to Lane, he discussed the matter with Ellison, who explained he believed the two just needed to communicate more and operate with identical thinking. However, not long after Ellison made these statements, he and Lane agreed it was time to split up. Lane expected to move from one type of COO to another—from turnaround to two in a box, perhaps. Ellison obviously struggled with that transition. Search consultants who counsel COO candidates, and the candidates themselves, should recognize that CEOs who bring in a number two under certain conditions may, as conditions change, have a hard time redesigning the COO role to meet new demands.

In addition, if a COO is hired the CEO must be prepared to publicly back and reinforce the COO's authority. Though the CEO-COO configuration may be born with good intentions, there are some who will try to ignore the implications of the arrangement. Specifically, executives whose reporting line to the CEO has been altered are normally the most upset. The CEO must explain to these executives that they must now take guidance from the COO. These executives often try to circumvent the new structure; they try to continue working directly with the CEO through a back door. The CEO must prevent this circumnavigation and close all the back doors, visibly supporting the new COO's authority. The CEO can still have an open door policy and be entirely accessible to the staff; however, once it is time to make a decision that falls in the purview of the number two, the CEO must push it down 100 percent of the time, without exception. Many CEOs do not realize the effort required to do this without bruising egos or otherwise aggravating key members of the team. The CEO must invest energy to prevent the departure of any key executive, sell the concept of a CEO-COO configuration, and get the executives to agree to work with the new number two.

As an example, although there were probably many reasons Disney's Eisner-Ovitz configuration did not work it is true that Eisner did little to sell Ovitz to his key staff, some of whom made it clear they would not be taking direction from Ovitz. Thus, during the search process CEOs should begin soft-selling the CEO-COO concept, explaining how critical it is as a driver of strategy and how it can help every key executive be more successful. After all, the decision to create a COO role is a significant strategic and structural change; an investment in generating recognition of the need to change and commitment for the change is as true here as it is of change efforts anywhere.

The Search from the Perspective of the Candidate

The prospective COO has a number of responsibilities throughout the search process as well. Clearly one important task is to understand, to the extent possible, how well the CEO and the company have planned the process. COO candidates must enter the process with ego in check, prepared to put the company and the CEO before themselves, should they eventually get the job. A key challenge for COOs who tend to have aspirations for greater things is to not look past the COO position to the chief executive's seat. Even when the motivation for creation of the COO role is succession planning, the COO should be brought in with the understanding that the CEO is in charge. A second ego-related challenge for new COOs is the ability to continuously and selflessly implement what may often be someone else's strategy and vision. This too is a matter that requires reflection and careful consideration on the part of the COO candidate. The ability to embrace and implement the CEO's vision and strategy can be particularly difficult for an accomplished executive. This reinforces the importance of two things: first, the COO candidate must view the

CEO as someone he or she respects and wants to work for; second, the CEO and COO must to some degree be similar-minded about the firm's future and the COO's evolving responsibilities. To the degree that their vision overlaps, this concern about the COO being forced to sublimate personal preferences is reduced. Ray Lane's words of caution capture both the need of the COO prospect to anticipate what working with the CEO will be like and the caution of understanding the importance of focusing on that role quite well:

> I would strongly advise any COO candidate to do all they can to explore what working with the CEO will be like. They need to think very carefully about how that relationship will evolve. They have to think about whether or not they are going to be able to be a partner to the CEO. They need to be convinced that they will be satisfied with the reality that the CEO is going to take credit when there is credit and he is going to deflect all the bad stuff to them. These are important things to consider.
>
> Unfortunately, some executives who take a COO job are primarily concerned about how well positioned they will then be towards becoming CEO. I think that is a poor motivation to accept a COO role. When considering the position at Oracle, that possibility was never on my mind. I just never envisioned retiring from Oracle as the CEO. Instead, I evaluated the position from the standpoint of how much I would be excited about going to work each day. I was focused on how well I felt I could perform *this* job—I wasn't distracted by thoughts of how much I might like the job that this one might lead me to.

The COO candidate must understand that the position may be the most complex and least understood role in the organization. Though many managers face the struggle of leading and following at the same time, the COO does so quite publicly. COOs must subordinate their ego and understand that in many cases success in their efforts will be attributed to the CEO, and though it may be done less publicly they should also be prepared to accept the blame for shortcomings. Moving from the chief executive role to the number two role can be a risky proposition for an executive because of the signal it sends to the market and because as a number two they may find themselves in a situation where they have accountability without full authority, which is always challenging. Thus the COO candidate should consider whether he or she is up to the challenges of this unique role and enter the search process with eyes wide open.

COO candidates, like the CEO of the hiring company, must invest time during the process to ensure philosophical alignment with regard to strategy and vision. If there is severe misalignment, the relationship will not work. As noted, Ed Zander knew it was time to leave Sun Microsystems as the COO when he realized that he and CEO Scott McNealy were diverging significantly on the vision for the company. A certain philosophical bedrock must exist; otherwise, behavior will reflect differences, the organization will potentially interpret those differences unproductively, and the business will suffer. At its worst are diverging strategies between the number one and two and an ensuing battle for control that paralyzes the company and leads to one or both executives exiting. This usually takes some time before it comes to a head, which can create camps; people leave the company and competitors use the events to get an advantage.

COO candidates must realize that the executives who reported directly to the CEO may resent creation of an additional layer of management that limits their direct access to the CEO. Navigating this situation requires a strong ability to build relationships. Newly minted COOs cannot be authoritative with these executives or operate from positional authority. In fact, they must rely

---

FOR COO SUCCESS, THE CANDIDATE MUST:

- *Have complete confidence that the CEO is excellent*
- *Quickly establish a deep mutual trust with the CEO*
- *Be comfortable working in an environment characterized by uncertainty and ambiguity*
- *Be effective at leading from strategy to execution*
- *Be comfortable making difficult, irreversible decisions*
- *Be comfortable with credit going to the top*
- *Quickly establish himself or herself as credible with other members of top management and the employees*
- *Be able to influence without the ultimate authority*
- *Be a quick study of people and situations*
- *Have deep industry knowledge*

heavily on influence and persuasion skills to achieve results, relying on executives whose work history and first allegiance are with the CEO. Further, they must demonstrate to these executives that they are an asset to them and good for the organization. In addition, the COO must demonstrate strong *followership* while fostering *leadership* in specific areas of responsibility. Ego subordination is critical here. According to Bill Nuti, former COO and then CEO of Symbol Technologies (now CEO at NCR), the COO must facilitate connectivity between these executives and the CEO, rather than shutting off their access. It is somewhat contradictory, as we have made clear, that the CEO must try to redirect these executives back to the COO. In this way, though, the transition is eased for all parties and the COO is more welcomed by key executives in the organization. As Nuti explained in Chapter Four, the most critical skill is listening: One has to "listen very clearly and have courage, the courage to listen over periods of time and not . . . jump in with a solution on day one because you think you know better or because the place you came from did it a certain way. You have to be an extremely good listener" and acknowledge the past in order to move toward the future.

Finally, though in many cases the COO is the implied or explicit CEO-apparent, a COO should never be a ceremonial post or a holding-pattern role. As explained previously, the decision to add a COO must be driven by good business strategy. Thus the COO candidate must realize he or she is being recruited to do a job, not just preparing to take the corner office. The COO should not try to accelerate the transition to the CEO role. Instead, COOs must focus on the duties they were recruited to perform.

The Search from the Perspective of the Recruiter

An external COO search is difficult to execute, and a search consultant cannot afford to perform merely transactionally. The key responsibility of the search firm in the process is to anticipate and then develop strategies to mitigate any threat that might derail the search. All too often, a search consultant begins a COO project by thinking about potential candidates to attract. The problem is the consultant is skipping the first step of the process: Was the decision to go to search well made in the first place? As we have argued, creation of the COO position is best driven by strategy. By challenging the CEO's thinking on pursuing a number two, the search consultant can help validate the reasons for doing so and also learn a great deal about the client company's strategy, as well as the key characteristics of the CEO and the senior team. As a result, the search consultant is not only much more likely to complete a search assignment successfully but also to prevent derailment of the newly appointed COO. After all, clients no longer are satisfied with an A placement; they want an A placement who stays on board for a while, adding value continuously.

Yet there are a host of derailment factors threatening to wreck the CEO-COO configuration and destroy shareholder value in the process. We discuss a number of them next.

Warning Signs That the Selection Is Failing

Though there are a number of derailment issues that threaten at any time, their impact can be mitigated. Here are common derailment factors and how the search consultant can mitigate the risk of each one by working to ensure ongoing engagement and commitment of the individuals involved.

The CEO Is Seeking a COO for the Wrong Reasons

Ironically, the best search consultants begin a proposed search project by challenging the decision to go to search in the first place. We have noted that the decision to bring in a number two should be made only after establishing a clear link between corporate strategy and the CEO-COO configuration. The search consultant must therefore fully understand the client's strategy. He or she should determine, with the CEO, whether a COO will help achieve the goals of the strategy or simply be perceived as an encumbrance. In addition to discovering the strategic link, the search consultant must understand the CEO's motivations for seeking a number two. The consultant, having developed an understanding of the strategic goals for the business, should be prepared to play devil's advocate, challenging the CEO to clearly articulate the advantages of a CEO-COO configuration, given the direction in which the CEO wants to take the business. Hambrick and Cannella discovered in one sample that a CEO-COO configuration correlates with underperformance vis-à-vis industry peers. It is critical to embark on this arrangement for the right business reasons.

As enumerated earlier in this book, logical reasons for pursuing the CEO-COO configurations include succession planning, a turnaround situation, new strategic initiatives, a dynamic industry, an operationally intensive business, and others. The search consultant should consider these typologies in evaluating the starting point for a COO search assignment. For example, Bill Swanson was initially brought into Raytheon as president of Electronic Systems, a $9 billion global business that was a key part of Raytheon. This gave him the opportunity to run a large, complex business in a lower-profile role than the number two job. It enabled him to learn the culture and build key relationships so that in 2003 he could step into the official number two role for a brief period and move into the CEO role before the end of that year. This successful process (Raytheon shares have gained steadily since mid-2003 despite tumult in the aerospace industry) is due in large part to Raytheon and then-CEO Dan Burnham selecting a CEO-designate for a strategic reason (namely, succession) and then planning key roles that leveraged Swanson's skill set and gave him ample opportunity to demonstrate results while gaining broad perspective on the entire enterprise as well as enhancing his visibility and relationships with the board of directors.

The CEO Is Not Ready

Often, CEOs intellectually understand the demands of a CEO-COO configuration; however, many do not fully appreciate the reality of longer days, greater time commitment, and increased sensitivity as to how their behavior is perceived. The search consultant must ensure the CEO fully understands that bringing on a COO will put more pressure on his or her time in the short run, as the CEO will need to ensure the success of the COO. This is really a matter of educating CEOs, taking them through the various scenarios that require their involvement and guidance. They do not always realize the implications of sharing power and authority over the long run.

For example, the search consultant must make sure the CEO really gets to know the COO candidate. In the Raytheon example, the number two came in not as the COO but in another large, complex role, and the CEO got to know him (to a certain degree) on the job before moving him into the COO/CEO-designate role. The two other examples are Kevin Rollins at Dell, where he began as head of U.S. operations, and Ray Lane at Oracle, who filled the same role as Rollins before moving into the number two post. Another possibility is recruiting someone the CEO has worked with in the past, as when John W. Thompson, the CEO of Symantec recruited John Schwartz, whom he had worked with at IBM. The level of familiarity with the culture and strategy was great for all of these executives by the time they moved into the on-deck circle. In another example, when Joe Leonard, the CEO of AirTran, began looking for a number two, he arrived at Robert Fornaro as the solution, partly because the two had worked together previously at Northwest Airlines and he knew his values and competencies from that previous experience. You can decrease the probability of COO derailment by working with a known quantity where you already have a relationship and understand the person's capabilities and values. This is not always possible. The search consultant must insist that the CEO invest a great deal of time during the search process to really get to know the candidate. Ultimately, the CEO must be prepared to share the most critical and sensitive information and the most visible signs of authority with someone else. The search consultant should force the CEO to think about the symbols of power and respect that exist within the company's values and culture (for example, product development at Oracle and Microsoft). If the CEO cannot imagine allowing the number two to control these functions visibly or make decisions in these groups with authority, then the CEO is probably not ready for a COO.

The Chemistry Is Wrong

As discussed, the search consultant should invest in getting to know the CEO on the level of values. Personal fit and chemistry between the CEO and COO are critical, and the search consultant must begin the search assignment with complete knowledge of the CEO's style and values. Craig Weatherup is vehement about the importance of chemistry between the number one and the number two. At PepsiCo, he and CEO Roger Enrico knew each other extremely well because earlier in their careers they both were stationed in Asia when it was tough and unglamorous to be there. These early bonding experiences enabled them to trust one another and work effectively together later when they were in the number one and two roles. In some cases, however, ego gets in the way. Sometimes CEOs are unwilling to share glory and COOs set out to establish themselves as the de facto number one. The search consultant must evaluate the egos and pursue candidates accordingly.

The COO Role Is Poorly Defined

The search consultant should play a key role in defining the COO's role and decision-making authority. This helps set candidate expectations up front and forces the CEO to think in detailed fashion about what he or she is willing to give up. In the due diligence phase, it is absolutely critical that a lot of time be spent on clearly defining the new content of the CEO and COO positions. This helps set up the entire process for success because it transcends the number one and two and communicates to the entire organization where authority for each element of the organization lies.

When Mort Topfer was recruited to Dell, it was not to serve as the CEO-designate or to free founder Michael Dell to play a few more rounds of golf. Topfer was brought in primarily to mentor Dell, a young founder-CEO. Topfer had no designs on the CEO spot, and it was made clear by the search consultant, John Thompson, that this would be a mentorship situation. Though the case study data were sparse on such a situation, the search consultant worked with Dell to clearly define what this would entail. When Topfer emerged as a leading candidate, the search consultant held frank discussion about the role. Topfer began coming on board almost three months before he retired from Motorola. He and Dell met regularly, and Topfer attended a number of meetings at his future employer's. In many cases, an executive as successful as Topfer would grow restless and might look past current responsibilities to the CEO's chair. However, having been brought into the process by a search consultant who was open and honest and had full understanding of the situation, the relationship worked quite well. In fact, Topfer eventually became invaluable as a mentor to Kevin Rollins, who actually was brought in as the head of U.S. operations, later became COO, and is now the CEO. The one-two configuration still exists at Dell (though titles have been elevated, with Michael in the chairman role). Topfer knew you had to be successful as a number two before you could be number one, and he knew what it took to be successful as a number two. It seems that Topfer's mentorship paid off: The Dell-Rollins CEO-COO configuration corresponded with an almost 30 percent share price increase over twenty-four months, while the DOW and NASDAQ were roughly flat. In 2004, Rollins moved seamlessly into the CEO slot.

Before Larry Ellison and Ray Lane parted ways, Oracle was a good example of setting a clear strategy that required a strong number two, and abiding by that strategy. When Lane was recruited into Oracle, he began as the president of U.S. operations before becoming the number two. This was a turnaround situation that required intense focus on certain operating elements of the business. Once Ray "fixed" operations in the United States, his role expanded and he became global COO, a role in which he enjoyed continued success (Oracle shares grew from under $2 in 1992 to roughly $40 when Lane left in 2000). Lane joined at a time when Oracle could immediately apply his expertise to solve a business problem that was critical to the overarching strategy. He was able to make quick gains in the U.S. business, which earned him credibility while giving him broad insight into the business. By the time he stepped into the COO role, the transition was natural and obvious, and his success was much more likely.

It is critical that the COO make clear his or her expectations. Failure to do so can cause a great deal of frustration, if not derailment. In Chapter Four we heard from Nuti, who joined a technology company as COO, that new COOs must be transparent as to their own career goals, whether those goals involve the opportunity to rise to the CEO position or the desire to serve as COO for the foreseeable future. In each case, the COO and the CEO need to understand the succession plan.

The Skill Overlap Is Too Great

It is critical that the CEO and COO share authority, but not necessarily responsibilities. In fact, the CEO-COO configuration is often more effective when the responsibilities—and thus the skills—are complementary and not redundant. To the extent that CEO and COO capabilities and proclivities overlap, there is a risk of friction and second-guessing. Together, these are threats that may lead to derailment of the number two. Nuti was recruited by John Thompson to be the president and COO at Symbol Technologies, with a clear charge to drive operational effectiveness across the organization. He had no illusions about his immediate role. According to Nuti, "I was Mr. Inside and the CEO was Mr. Outside."

The search consultant must invest time to learn the CEO's core competencies and begin the search from this point. The COO's skills should be complementary and without too much overlap. If the CEO and COO have too much overlap, they will focus on many of the same elements of the strategy as they naturally gravitate to their strengths. This leads to duplication of effort, which yields frustration and perception on the part of the organization that the two are not in sync.

Lack of Communication

"Communication is absolutely critical," says Craig Weatherup, who served as COO at PepsiCo. Ongoing feedback, according to Bill Nuti, must be "constant. Mind-numbing. And very transparent." The CEO and COO must force regular communication in the form of sync-up meetings, phone calls, and strategy sessions. They must also interact informally. Mort Topfer and Kevin Rollins physically located their offices next to each other so they could interact more frequently and easily. This also sent the message to Rollins of how important communication was when working with Michael Dell.

The On-Boarding Process Is Vague

In some cases, the number two is the "eventual COO" and brought on in a role that is smaller in scope or scale. Such a situation allows the new executive to learn with less scrutiny, bite off a smaller piece, and achieve a quick win by focusing intensely on a smaller piece. It also causes less disruption among those who directly report to the CEO; they see this new person not as the COO right away, and with the person getting quick wins he or she is perceived as earning the COO role. Such a tactic represents an effective process for coming on board. An example of success in this regard is Jim Donald, who was named CEO of Starbucks in March 2005. When he joined Starbucks as president of North America, he had already been a successful chief executive at Pathmark Stores. However, he wanted the opportunity to lead as the CEO in a larger organization in a unique industry. Because he was used to leading as the top executive, this would be a high-risk proposition. There were no guarantees, but Donald was willing to make the move. He began as president of North America and contributed significantly to the company's impressive share growth from late 2002 to early 2005. Once he became CEO, he already knew the business (especially the core markets), the partners, and the strategy; when Orin Smith handed over the reins, it was a surprise to no one.

Board's Role Is Not Addressed in the Search Process

Though our interviews showed variation in the depth of the relationship between the COO and the board, in every case there was at least a reasonable amount of interaction between the two. It was rare to find a COO with a board seat; companies pointed to the recent emphasis on independent, external board members. In some instances, the COO played a role serving on a board committee; in others the COO regularly presented to the board; and in still others the COO attended the part of a board meeting viewed as relevant to his or her responsibilities. In each case, however, it is clear that the COO and the board interact, so it is important that the board be comfortable with the COO from the outset. Clearly, this is most critical—and surely most easily accom-

---

QUESTIONS A PROSPECTIVE COO SHOULD ASK

- *Is the CEO excellent?*
- *Is the CEO ready to invest in my success?*
- *Has a compelling business case for the COO position been developed and disseminated?*
- *Does the board support the business case for the COO position?*
- *Has sufficient attention been paid to defining the boundaries of the COO position?*
- *Can I foresee developing a close, trusting relationship with the CEO?*
- *What is the CEO's leadership style, and how well will it work for me?*
- *What are my career goals and aspirations, and how is this opportunity going to be instrumental in achieving those goals at this time?*
- *How strong is the top management team, and to what extent have they bought into the COO position?*
- *Have the CEO and the board demonstrated and communicated a clear message regarding my role in the succession plans?*

plished—when the COO has been hired as the heir apparent. Succession planning is a mission-critical role for a board of directors, and they must partner with the CEO and search consultant to ensure the role is being created for the correct reasons, help vet candidates, and assist in the installation and ongoing growth of the number two.

Naturally, the first place that board involvement makes sense is during the decision process surrounding whether or not to create such a position. The board can play a key role up front challenging the CEO's rationale in creating a number two role. Is there a business imperative or is this simply for comfort or to try to retain someone who may never ascend to the top job? The board has a fiduciary responsibility to challenge the CEO to ensure the best decision is being made both in creating the role and selecting the individual, whether internal or external.

It is important to recognize that board members can play a role in attracting and hiring the best COO candidate by making themselves available and acting as another source of information on the company strategy and key issues. As the new COO joins the company, board members can also help the new COO by assigning a director to the newly hired COO. The director can act as a mentor to provide help as the COO navigates key issues at the board level, as well as support with other aspects of this new role.

SUMMARY

We suggest that there are two key lessons in this chapter. First, it is important to be cognizant of the critical role played by the CEO in attracting, recruiting, bringing on board, and continuously managing the COO. A second critical take-away concerns developing appreciation for the complexity of establishing a fit between the COO and both the CEO and the larger organization. There is pressure to ensure a good fit between these two executives with regard to trust and communication, and there is an issue of COO fit with the rest of the organization as well. Does the COO seem suited to the company culture? If a dysfunctional or otherwise inappropriate culture is part of the business case for bringing on a COO, is there evidence the COO can get the job done? Do the capabilities of the COO candidate fit the short-term and likely long-term demands of the COO position? Do the career aspirations and timetable of the

COO and career opportunities at the company seem reasonably in sync? In all, this notion of fit is clearly a multidimensional problem; there are many aspects. This leads to a vexing question: If an organization cannot maximize fit on each of the many important dimensions, some of which are quite nuanced, is there an understanding of where compromise can be made without jeopardizing the success of the position?

The key conclusion is that creating a number two role is a strategic decision for the company and should not be taken lightly. It is critical that the CEO and board challenge the notion of why the role is being considered and whether it makes sense in the current evolution and strategic priorities of the company. Once there is agreement on the business imperatives and the need for a number two, the real work begins. The company's leadership needs to select a qualified search consultant to partner with them and challenge their thinking and perspectives—someone who is not looking for a warm body but wants instead to understand their strategy, culture, and imperatives and will look for the correct match across all of the continua. The CEO must be pushed to understand his or her key role in the process and the huge investment of time up front during the due diligence phase, during the on-boarding, and throughout the number two's tenure. They need to be introspective, willing to pass on power and decision-making authority, and comfortable doing so. If the CEO is not ready to do this, he or she is not ready for a number two.

In all, adding a COO position to an organizational structure is in many ways analogous to acquiring a business. As such, the decision should be driven by strategy, with a goal of value creation for the business. Effective execution of such a decision begins with a thorough due diligence process on the part of the company and the candidate; throughout, commitment and dedication are required to ease the process. For these reasons, "acquiring" a COO—like acquisition of a business or a group of assets—means an increase in effort by the CEO if the acquisition is to create value. Part of the CEO's job is always to develop a likely successor; the expectation is often that the COO is this person. If this is the case, the CEO has to be deliberate about exposing the COO to the board and other important constituents, early and often. Whether or not the COO is a likely successor, this standing needs to be clearly communicated to those involved.

From the COO's perspective, the arrangement should be treated more like a merger than an acquisition, in that he or she has a great deal of responsibility for making it work. The COO cannot expect the CEO (or an acquiring company) to solely manage the integration or determine where and how the COO will add value. The COO must work to ensure success and the best use of his or her intellectual assets. Together, the CEO and the COO must make sure that there is ongoing agreement as to the boundaries of one another's position and that these boundaries are widely understood.

NOTE

1. See Kenneth W. Freeman's contribution in the *Harvard Business Review* for an excellent summary of the issues in succession: The CEO's Real Legacy. (2004, November). *Harvard Business Review.*

A CONVERSATION WITH VINCENT C. PERRO

GLOBAL MANAGING PARTNER, LEADERSHIP SERVICES, HEIDRICK AND STRUGGLES
FORMERLY COO OF NEXTERA ENTERPRISES

Vincent C. Perro is Heidrick and Struggles's global managing partner in leadership consulting, responsible for the firm's talent management consulting services. He has built, grown, and led several global human capital, technology, and strategy consulting businesses. Before joining Heidrick and Struggles in 2004, he headed up Sibson Consulting, a leading human capital consulting firm. Previously, he was COO and a board member for Nextera Enterprises, a publicly held multiline consulting firm. Prior to that, he was with then-independent Sibson & Co., where he held numerous leadership positions, including president of Sibson International, chair of the board of Sibson & Co., and financial services practice leader. His earlier work experience was in senior line and staff roles for a major Wall Street firm (http://www.heidrick.com/Experience/Consultants/ConsultantDetail.aspx?ConsultantCode=14915).

AUTHORS: Tell us about your transition into the COO role at Nextera Enterprises.

PERRO: I came into the role in 2000. It was a role that had been unoccupied for a while. I was an internal move into this position and had been running the international business from one of the units. At the time, this whole business was a four-consulting-division company with operations in the United States, Europe, and Australia. We were about a $200 million company but had very little in the way of centralized capabilities. The company was originally envisioned as more of a holding company, and the reason I was asked to come on board was because the board had decided that we needed to integrate the businesses and all of the supporting operations. We also had a single controlling investor, which made investor relations a bit different than usual. The CEO spent most of his time dealing with the investor. I was charged with running the business day-to-day.

AUTHORS: From your experience as COO, what first comes to your mind as the competencies necessary for success in the role?

PERRO: As I noted, I came into the role in 2000. It was the end of the dot com bubble, so we went from this frantic acquisition mode to rapid retrenchment with cutbacks, downsizing, and ultimately divestitures. There was no such thing as a normal operating experience during my time in the COO role.

In light of the environment, one of the most important things during that time was to give people confidence that the changes under way were not going to be harmful to them—which is especially critical for a consulting business that depends on the confidence of its producers. Communicating about the rapid changes we were experiencing and showing how these changes could provide opportunities to realize their vision for the company: That was the first priority.

The second challenge was to convince them that in order to execute this strategy and survive the coming downturn, some old ways needed to change. When I came to the role, there were separate accounting groups, separate HR groups, separate marketing groups, and so on. These separate groups needed to be integrated.

The third priority was persuading people that the vision in fact could be implemented. Whenever there is change or turmoil, this is critical. We brought in a new CEO shortly after I became COO, so another one of my jobs was to help the new CEO gain trust by advising him on the culture, personalities, and histories of the operating units.

So in all, communication skills, change management, the ability to communicate a vision and develop commitment to the vision—those were skills I needed to display.

AUTHORS: Talk a little bit about the relationship between the number one and the number two. Is friction between the two inevitable?

PERRO: I think there is going to be a little bit of friction no matter what, because people at this level have strong views and to some degree the roles reinforce that. Though we certainly had our share, none were terribly dysfunctional and we managed to deal with them effectively. A clear definition of roles helped. When I went into the job, the incumbent CEO did not want to get involved in operational matters. The CEO who later joined us had a little more of a hands-on orientation. In the beginning he wanted to dig into more of the details than made sense. It took us a while to sort it out, but it turned out well.

The executives running the business units and also the big producers liked to "pick their court." Sometimes they would come to me; sometimes they would come to the CEO depending on where they thought they would get the most favorable audience for their issue. The CEO and I constantly communicated on these issues and the decisions or views we had so that we were not set off one against the other. In general, he deferred operational issues to me. It did not take long before people understood they could not play us off against each other.

AUTHORS: Is there time in the business life cycle or needs of the business where it makes sense to have a number two?

PERRO: For us, both the business cycle and our strategy were factors. When we first started the company, I don't think we needed a COO. There was a holding company and the COO was basically the CEO's administrator. It was very frustrating for him, and he eventually left. When I came in, we really did need a COO to integrate the business. We pulled out all of the functional units from the businesses and had them report to me. In addition, the rapid downturn of the business caused us to remove several of our business unit managers.

When that was necessary, I would go in and run it until we could get a new leader in place. However, to get the senior people engaged, my usual first step was to remove extra layers of management. While this was the right answer, it started to make my role a bit unworkable, so I wound up appointing a COO that could handle the more routine issues. In essence, I operated several business units as CEO while serving as the overall COO. This made sense because it was a time of crisis.

In a company where you have a new CEO, a COO is a pretty good thing to have. A COO can be very helpful, assuming the roles can be properly defined and the relationship between the two executives is a good one. In a company that is going through a very dramatic transition where you need a lot of implementation done, it is very useful. I also think that a smooth-running business where the CEO is focused on acquisitions is another good setting for a COO.

AUTHORS: **Does being COO prepare you properly to become a CEO?**

PERRO: Yes, but I think there are still gaps—some real, some perceived. During a lot of this time, I was doing multiple jobs. At any given time, I was COO of the whole business and acting CEO of one of the business units that was going through a change. I found that when I was in the business unit CEO role, I spent more time thinking strategically than I did in the COO role. A COO role doesn't give you as much opportunity to exercise that muscle. Also, you are insulated from the investor relations and capital structure issues. Fortunately, I was an inside board member, because we dealt with a lot of complex financial issues. I got good experience working on the corporate finance aspects of the CEO position. In addition, I always participated in the quarterly analyst calls and developed an appreciation of how to talk with the Street. When you are not on the board you can miss getting in-depth experience with these critical aspects of the CEO job. Fundamentally, I think those are the two real gaps: Often you are out of the loop on corporate finance and IR issues, and you probably don't get as much opportunity to dig into strategy.

On the perception side, you sometimes can be viewed as a little more transactional. As so often happens in business, you can become a captive of the role and find that people like to put labels on you that you then have to work hard to shed. However, when you have a structure with very strong, autonomous business units, the COO is going to be a weaker candidate for that top job than the CEO of a business unit. To me, the critical criterion for being a candidate for CEO is that you establish that you are bona fide in corporate finance side and strategy. If you have done that, then the experience as COO should put you ahead of the operating business unit heads.

AUTHORS: Is there a natural life span for a COO role?

PERRO: I have known well about a half-dozen COOs in various businesses over the years. Many of them have felt more endangered than their CEOs. Certainly, you are at risk of taking the blame if operational matters go seriously wrong. Other than that, I don't believe there is a natural life span for the role. More likely, there is a natural life span for the incumbent. Most that succeed are likely to want to step up to the CEO role before too long.

A CONVERSATION WITH DAN ROSENSWEIG

COO, YAHOO!

Daniel Rosensweig was appointed chief operating officer of Yahoo! in April 2002. He has responsibility for Yahoo!'s operations worldwide, including product development, marketing, international operations, and North American operations, which encompasses all of the company's operating units as well as advertising sales. Before coming to Yahoo!, Rosensweig was president of CNET Networks. Prior to that, he had an eighteen-year career at Ziff-Davis, where he served in many capacities, finally as president and chief executive officer of ZDNet (http://docs.yahoo.com/docs/pr/executives/rosensweig.html).

AUTHORS: What is important in regard to the decision to create a COO role?

ROSENSWEIG: In a very dynamic industry where there are a lot of moving parts, your company benefits from having the CEO focus on the next generation: analyzing where the business is going, what is around the corner, and which of all the innovations that are on the horizon will be most important to the company. At the same time, you also need somebody who is focused on executing the current vision: setting and meeting daily, quarterly, and annual goals; following up; making sure things happen. The COO needs to be driving the organization forward today, putting it in position to take advantage of new opportunities tomorrow. In my opinion, while there are people who can do one or the other of these jobs very well, you can't expect the same person to do a great job at both simultaneously. When looking at a company like Yahoo! that is in a dynamic, highly creative and competitive marketplace and is also growing incredibly fast, I think you would do a disservice to the company by having one person manage all of that. Having a COO position to keep the organization focused and executing is critical to success when there is significant complexity and rapid industry growth. Somebody needs to make sure that what we *say* is going to happen *is* in fact happening when, where, and how it is supposed to—or communicating when it isn't, and if needed they need to be able to fix it. Someone else needs to be saying, "Great, and where are we going next, how we are going to get there, and what do we need to accomplish it?"

AUTHORS: **In your description, the skill or competency set for the CEO and COO are reasonably different; the roles are different so the application of skills is different. You have an operationally intensive, execution-oriented number two who keeps things on track as well as a number one who is more visionary to provide a framework for success and a direction to drive towards.**

ROSENSWEIG: I think here at Yahoo!, where our roles are different, it follows that we use different yet complementary skills. That said, having the skills and having the time to apply all of those skills are different matters. That is why creating both roles is desirable. I think that there are people in positions like mine who aspire to have the CEO job. To assume that there is a unique set of skills for CEO that is completely independent of those for COO would suggest that a CEO could never have been a COO. That may be the case with certain individuals in certain companies, but I don't think that necessarily has to be the case.

AUTHORS: **Looking at it another way, how well does the number two position prepare someone to be a CEO?**

ROSENSWEIG: It could, and it certainly gives you a platform to be considered for the job. However, it certainly doesn't assure it. If the company is moving in a direction that demands the skill set and vision held by the number two, then of course. And learning from a great chairman and chief executive about how to think about where the company needs to go and how to develop strategies that can be realized operationally can give you a fair shot at that position. On the other hand, everything depends, as it always does, on the job, on the role, the current circumstances, and on passion. Passion is essential to drive companies and people into new business and the unknown. Even leaders want to be led in that when you are creating industries; you have to have passion to drive you through the inevitable obstacles and doubt. Where it doesn't put you in the position is when the CEO and COO roles are so completely separate, where somebody focuses solely on the day-to-day as opposed to also thinking about where the company is going and where to bridge the gap. So as you might expect, it depends on the individual, the job, and the circumstances.

AUTHORS: In your mind, is there a life span to being the number two? Is it "too late" in a sense to move to a CEO job After a certain period of time?

ROSENSWEIG: Again, I think it depends on the individual. If you take the COO job with the expectation to be the number one, you probably shouldn't have taken the job in the first place. The focus of the COO is to execute on the vision of the CEO and provide a positive environment for success, not lobbying to be the CEO. So if you are thinking about your next role, you really aren't doing your job. There are lots of other jobs where you can think about lots of other things, but not when you are the chief *operating* officer. Second of all, it is mistake to stay in the job if you actually think that you should have the CEO job versus the person in it. If you don't have confidence in the leader, you should get out of that job. Now, if you continue to believe in the leader's vision, the company's opportunities, that you are making a significant contribution to the success and future of the organization, and if you are learning and having a good time, then the life span is as long as you are still engaged and interested in performing. A third case is if you feel that at a certain point it is important to you, the individual, to run a company and be the top person and that opportunity is not going to present itself where you are, either because the CEO intends to stay or maybe the board doesn't consider you the logical next choice. Then you should go. I don't think I agree with what I have read before that people shouldn't stay in the job more than four years because people pigeon-hole you as the number two. I think individuals make their own circumstances and opportunities. I also don't think any situation is necessarily the same as another.

AUTHORS: **We talked to Kevin Sharer, the CEO of Amgen. He was president and COO for seven years. He said when he went into the role he had no conception that it could last that long. But he said he and the CEO had a great relationship, he learned everything and continued to grow in the role, and it just made sense to go to seven years.**

ROSENSWEIG: I think that is exactly right. Again, I think when you are creating a company you have to establish and articulate clear roles and responsibilities for key staff members. It follows that the person in the COO role would also set goals for himself or herself. The primary goal I set for myself, or how I define what success looks like for me, is to be working at a company that matters, as well as making a meaningful impact with someone who I think affects positive change. I also want to be providing a benefit to my family, and a big part of that benefit is enjoying myself. Why would I put a limitation on my enjoyment? There is an old view on Wall Street, which is: they love you until they don't. For me, I am going to stay happy until I am not. In other words, I'm not putting a time limit on my happiness either.

AUTHORS: **That sounds like something Yogi Berra would say. You and a few others have talked about happiness in the role. Kevin at Amgen said the same thing; he said he was having a blast.**

ROSENSWEIG: I get to work for a guy like Terry Semel [chairman and CEO]. I also get to work with partners like Sue Decker [CFO] and Farzad Nazem [CTO], who are leaders in their fields, as well as visionaries like Jerry Yang and David Filo [co-founders and chief Yahoos]. What isn't great about that? I am old enough to know at this point in my life that the grass isn't always greener. I am also old enough to know and to recognize what is a really good, positive, constructive situation. It's like what I teach my children: Good things are good things—enjoy them.

AUTHORS: What about your direct reports? How do you design who reports to the CEO versus who reports to the number two?

ROSENSWEIG: Truthfully, you do that in conjunction with the CEO. There is a very simple default: Functions that the CEO thinks are important to have directly reporting to him or her should report to him or her. You really shouldn't question that. A lot about life is how you build relationships and trust, and if you feel that you can't be successful working for somebody in the way that they feel they need to be successful, then you should not be there. I think it is the job of the number two to find a way to be successful in the structure that the CEO prefers, assuming the CEO has a preference. Again, if you put the company first, and the assumption is the most important link in the chain is the chairman and the CEO, then everything cascades from that. Most important for success is to establish a world of constant communications, clear roles, trust, and a clear definition of what success looks like. If you do that, then the actual reporting lines can be less important.

AUTHORS: Is it hard to recruit people, the world's best people, if they have to report to the number two?

ROSENSWEIG: To execute and achieve success, you need a combination of thought leaders and executors, and to sustain success you need to combine the two in a team framework. I think if people's independent needs outside the role of the team become the priority, then it is harder for the team to achieve success. It is fine to have personal goals and ambitions, but as soon as they interfere with the company's agenda, it is time to go. There is only going to be one number one. That is pretty straightforward. There is only going to be a certain number of direct reports to that number one, and it's up to the team to find success within that framework. That doesn't mean it is the only way to be successful, but a team must be able to work within the agenda of the CEO. As a number two you must also establish yourself as a leader and earn your own credibility and clout, which means if you can't bring value to each of your direct reports you can't serve the CEO or the company effectively. And if my direct reports can't bring value to each of their direct reports, they shouldn't be in the job. To me, that just cascades down.

AUTHORS: What about new COOs who are coming in from the outside? Are there certain things they should do in their first six months, first ninety days, to come on board more successfully?

ROSENSWEIG: First, you have to get in sync with the CEO. If you have an agenda that is different than his or hers, you will absolutely fail the company. You need to spend a great deal of time being able to understand, embrace, and then be able to articulate and execute how you plan to achieve those goals. You spend a great deal of time on that. The second thing is to spend a great deal of time with your direct reports listening to how they think their role and their groups can achieve success for the company. If the team is not up to task, it is important to move fast, and to show the company you can make hard choices and good decisions. There are a few rules to live by. First, never be in a hurry to make a mistake. Second, don't make a decision until you are ready to make a decision. If you allow yourself to be forced into a decision that you are unprepared to make, you just have better odds of being wrong. Third, whatever decision you make, articulate it clearly and explain to people how they will be measured subsequent to that decision. You can't be a good leader saying "because I want you to do it." You have to be able to articulate the goals and what success looks like. Life is about selling the decision so people can get on board, enhance your decision, and create even greater success with it. And Terry is brilliant at that. In my case, as the number two, I make it happen.

AUTHORS: A lot of people who come into the number two role, and even those in the number one role who bring in a COO, may underestimate the investment they need to make together, up front, in the first six months, to make it successful at the back end.

ROSENSWEIG: Even before I started, I met with Terry several times for hours, just to listen. That was even before my first day. I think it is the job of the number two to build the bridge and the bond to the number one. My job is to put him in the best position to make the best decisions for the company. I don't think it's productive to sit back and wait for the CEO to spend his or her time figuring out how to make the COO successful, but rather it is the COO's job to figure out how to make the CEO and the company more successful. It's the kind of respect I would want to be afforded if I was in the number one position. And I think the number two must give that respect. After all, the company depends upon the success of the number one.

AUTHORS: In your time at Yahoo! to date, what stands out as special?

ROSENSWEIG: There have been a lot of great moments. I first joined the company when Yahoo! was still struggling to find its place—we were turning things around. The chairman and CEO had been there less than a year and was new to the industry. The CFO and CTO had stayed through the transition. And both founders were and are still active in the company. I was the new person on the block, hired to run the day-to-day operations. We had not yet begun to have success again. The first six months of the team coming together was very encouraging, exciting, and satisfying. Then we went on to have really vigorous, hard debates about whether we ought to be in certain businesses, how we ought to organize, whether we should make certain acquisitions, and whether we should take on certain competitive situations like Google and search engine companies. I think all of those things formed a lasting bond. We knew how to address the most difficult, complicated issues as a team. I think there were a lot of great lessons learned and that there were seminal moments. We learned important lessons about ourselves and about how to really debate difficult issues, such as where the company should go, who would be responsible for what, if we had the right people, and how we could set a tone of honesty, trust, and positive interaction. We learned that when people have a difference of opinion, we could discuss and disagree but then come together once a decision was made.

The other thing that is important for people to understand is that when you are the COO, your primary responsibility is to drive those decisions to success, whether you agreed with the decision or not. You can't allow yourself to have doubts or to show the team differences of opinion. Once the call has been made, you must own it, embrace it, and drive it to success like it is your own.

From that whole process, we know how to deal with the most difficult situations without politics or backstabbing. I think that comes from two things. It comes from the leadership at the top, and it comes from the individuals immediately below. And I think you can't have one or the other; everybody has to put the company first and learn to trust the other players on the team. One of the great lessons in life is if you have great talent you need to let them be successful the way they know how to be successful.

A CONVERSATION WITH BRUCE STEIN

FOUNDER AND MANAGING PARTNER OF THE HATCHERY
FORMERLY COO, MATTEL

The Hatchery is a family and kids entertainment and consumer products company. Prior to his efforts there, Bruce served as CEO/chairman of Radical Communication, where he successfully transformed a production-based communications company into an enterprise-class, full-service software provider with proprietary state-of-the-art technologies. Bruce also served as the worldwide president, COO, and board member to Mattel, a $5 billion world leader in children's toys and software. His role there included such responsibilities as marketing and development of all global toy and software product lines, financial management, and market distribution and partnership alliances across the company's global network. He previously held roles as CEO of Sony Interactive Entertainment and chief strategist of Sony Pictures Entertainment, consultant to DreamWorks SKG and Mandalay Entertainment, and president of the Kenner Products Division of Hasbro.

AUTHORS: What do you see as the critical competencies for a COO?

STEIN: In my view, there are certain things you have to assume as givens. One, obviously there must be sufficient gray matter there and you must have demonstrated proof of organizational leadership and coordination of teams. With those attributes in place, at least you have foundational elements. You then have to start considering if there is a demonstrated ability and inclination to execute strategic goals.

In some ways, the COO has to be the consummate plate spinner. Those plates include the day-to-day operations, achieving basic profit and revenue goals, dealing with personnel and operational details, etc. Equally important in the mix are spinning some larger plates, which make a strategic difference to the company. If all you have is someone who is comfortable with the process of managing operations, then perhaps you don't need the COO position. But if you do get someone that is comfortable with the multiple hats and on their own initiative will come up with their own plan of "Here are the things that, if I achieve in the next year, my business will be greatly improved," I think you have the right kind candidate.

Lastly, one of the things that I would stress is that the COO must be a courageous representative of the management of the company to the CEO and, equally importantly, to the board. You also have to be able to communicate a clear vision to the strategic partners of the company, as well as the Street, vendors, and company relationships, of that sort. There is no real good structure within board management for evaluating the COO contribution vis-à-vis the CEO. The CEO, understandably, has the board's ear and needs to have the support of the board. But the CEO and COO must clearly share a vision. If there are significant differences on strategic issues, then you likely have an indicator that the board has to take a more active role in understanding the issues in the company to effectively execute their jobs.

AUTHORS: What happens when the two come to a fork in the road? Does the COO have to leave the company?

STEIN: Maybe. It depends on the individuals, obviously. It should put the board on alert that the differences should be understood. The point that I was making is that there need to be adequate checks and balances within the operation of the company such that the board can really monitor a CEO's performance.

AUTHORS: What about the number two's role with the board? A couple of questions: (1) Should the COO sit on the board? And (2) how much interaction should the person have with the board?

STEIN: There are a number of initiatives as it relates to board function and responsibility that Sarbanes-Oxley is attempting to address. If as a result of these initiatives the board does have an accurate view of company operations, then I'm not sure a COO needs to sit on the board. But whether or not the COO sits on the board is less important than whether or not the board takes an active role in understanding the company management culture and the way management views their leadership. There is no substitute for doing that firsthand because the CEO's representation to the board will be biased by their own view, at a minimum. This can become especially problematic if the board is populated by members not well experienced in running the business, or a closely related business. In those cases, they often cannot effectively assess the

CEO's performance even if their intentions are there. Those are instances that would be helped by having a COO present to complete the picture of company operations presented by the CEO.

AUTHORS: So what else do you see as warning signs in CEO-COO relationships?

STEIN: It is hard to single out individual warning signs as each case will likely be different depending on the company and personalities. You really need to make sure that everybody is carrying the banner of the company and not their ego because someone that is egocentric will have a difficult time empowering others—a sure way to get the least out of your employees. Insecure, egocentric CEOs generally do better with a broad staff of reports without a COO inserting themselves into the mix. It doesn't necessarily mean they will be a bad CEO, it just means they probably are not the right person for a constructive relationship with a COO.

AUTHORS: You see a lot of derailment and the position not working well when the CEO creates the role but is not ready for it.

STEIN: When you asked about what doesn't work, just from an operational standpoint, it is real simple. If you find an organization where tactical approvals of COO decisions by the CEO are necessary or you have CEO micromanagement of operational details, you are breeding inefficiency, and it is a silent organizational killer. It costs time, money, and maybe most importantly it uselessly expends the intellectual capital of the rest of the company because people are motivated to find answers the CEO wants and not those that necessarily improve the business. When you set up the structure it should be objectively apparent that the responsibilities for a COO are X and for the CEO are Y and both want those jobs. And they both truly want both jobs filled and working well together. There are CEOs who claim to want a strong COO but in the end are too threatened by their role in the company to let them succeed.

AUTHORS: Does the number two role properly prepare you to be the number one?

STEIN: Well, that is an interesting question because there isn't a single set of attributes that come with every COO package. Managed properly and with an eye on preserving shareholder value, the COO is an excellent place for the organization to build bench strength and ultimately a back-up for the CEO. If an exceptional COO is in place behind a CEO, then the worst that you risk is that somebody else will come along and pick off the COO before they replace the CEO, and that training is gone. I believe that is not just worth the risk but also the responsibility of management and the board to make sure the CEO has a great back-up. If the COO leaves, the board ought to be certain to do an exit interview to understand the reasons for the departure, or they have no chance of increasing the odds that the next COO will stay.

A CONVERSATION WITH MORT TOPFER

MANAGING DIRECTOR, CASTLETOP CAPITAL
FORMERLY VICE CHAIRMAN, DELL INC.

Mort Topfer is managing director and co-founder of Castletop Capital, an investment firm headquartered in Austin, Texas, and founder and chairman of the Topfer Family Foundation. Previously, he was vice chairman of Dell from 1994 to 2000 and is currently a member of the board of directors of Staktek Holdings and Measurement Specialties. He moved to the Austin area after a twenty-three-year career at Motorola, where he held several key leadership positions. His professional accomplishments include a Dell manufacturing campus in his name, as well as a Darjah Johan Negeri Penang State Award presented to him by the governor of Penang in recognition of his efforts to expand the electronics industry in Malaysia (http://www.matff.org/mort.htm).

AUTHORS: Please tell us about your role at Dell.

TOPFER: When Michael decided to bring someone in, it was a very young company with a lot of young, highly ambitious people. One of the concerns he had was even though I was fifty-eight years old, he didn't really want to create a structure where all these young guys felt that I would be a barrier to their continued career advancement. The interesting thing is the people in the company had great apprehension about this fifty-eight-year-old guy coming from an "old days" company like Motorola into a very entrepreneurial environment. It was not a problem, but I talked to lots of people and there was a lot of apprehension about that. I did not change. I went to work with a shirt and tie every day for at least two or three years before I slowly evolved into a less formal kind of attire. He chose the vice chairman title and that worked fine with me. We basically went in a kind of co-leadership role in running the company. As the company grew and unfolded, we abandoned that structure. In fact, when Kevin Rollins first joined the office of the CEO, he was also a vice chairman. As I phased out of the company, we made Kevin president and COO. Recently he took over the CEO title. But through all these transitions and titles, the roles of the people who participated in the chairman's office never really changed. There were clearly defined areas of responsibility and focus. The titles have changed to more represent what we thought was the right interface between the outside world and the inside world.

AUTHORS: You mention the importance of clearly defined roles and responsibilities. How does that best get decided and communicated to others?

TOPFER: Before I even took the job with Michael, we spent probably two or three months discussing this. While I don't think it should be taken as the letter of the law, I think each of the parties in a shared office need to feel free to go anywhere and do anything. At the same time, defined areas of focus and responsibility help direct reports to keep more structure in things. Quite frankly, I think the most important part of any kind of shared role is having two people who have complementary skills, mutual respect, and very open dialogue with each other so both know exactly what is going on throughout the company. Otherwise, I think barriers that create strategy problems will inevitably develop and execution problems will occur.

AUTHORS: One of the roles that you played was as a mentor role to a young CEO-founder. Can you talk about how you were able to help him grow professionally as a CEO and a founder?

TOPFER: The interesting thing is, as everyone knows, he actually hired me to be his mentor. That was kind of the role that we described and talked about. It evolved into really running the company jointly, the challenges the company faced, and I think that the needed changes in the leadership and the company required my role to change over time. When I originally joined the company, it was really not in the role that I really moved into, after only about three or four months, and that occurred as Michael and I continued to dialogue and face the challenges the company faced and then evolved into that role.

AUTHORS: You talked about communication being critical. How often did you meet and sort of align to make sure you were always shoulder to shoulder on the issues?

TOPFER: Dell, like a lot of other companies today, runs on e-mail. I would say we probably e-mailed each other multiple times every day and we probably spent time together every day when we were both in the office at the same time. If you in fact would visit Dell today—it is interesting, I think this is going a little too far—but Michael and Kevin actually have offices that have a glass door separating them with a door that opens up. I think that is going a little too far, but I think it communicates the level of open dialogue that needs to occur to really keep a big dynamic company going in the same direction.

AUTHORS: Can you tell us a bit about the decision to have Kevin Rollins come on board?

TOPFER: I probably spent a year, a year and a half trying to get Kevin to join the company. Finally he accepted the job as head of the Americas. When I went to the board, there was a concern about—the Americas region was probably two-thirds of the revenue and probably 75 percent of the profits of the company—putting a consultant, if you will, into such a key role. So the board only agreed to him moving into that role with me remaining acting in that role. It only lasted three months because I went back to the board at the next meeting and said, "Why are we doing this sham? Kevin is in the role, he is doing the job; we ought to give him the title and make it official." And that is what we did. By the way, the interesting thing is the guy who raised the issue was Michael Jordan, who had come out of McKinsey, and he was the one who was concerned most about a consultant going into an operating role. He had troubles when he made the transition.

AUTHORS: Essentially, you came in and provided coaching and mentoring for Michael. You moved into more of an operating role and then at least for some period of time moved into sort of a coaching role for Kevin.

TOPFER: Sure, I was kind of the older statesman and Kevin and I actually—well, at the time when he joined the company he really reported to me and ran the Americas region. But about one year and a half after that, we moved him up to share the office with Michael and me, as I was really focused on grooming a replacement so I could retire someday.

AUTHORS: **You have mentioned coming in as the statesman and helping mentor Michael. One of the keys that enables this to work was likely the fact that there wasn't the threat that you were ever after his job.**

TOPFER: No—exactly, although up until just very recently Michael was reluctant to give up the CEO title. I encouraged him to do that probably two years ago or more because he needed to ensure locking Kevin in. Kevin was on everybody's radar screen for recruitment for CEO roles and there are a lot of people for whom having that title is meaningful. When I actually told Michael I wasn't going to stand for reelection last year about this time, then I think he started thinking through the process of making Kevin CEO—which we did in July when I stepped off the board—and Kevin filled my seat on the board.

AUTHORS: **How does decision making take place in this co-leader model? Dell is one example.**

TOPFER: Gates and Ballmer at Microsoft have done it well too, I think. I think again you have to work on it and you also have to have enough confidence in the relationship that you could speak your mind and take on the boss, like I had to do with Michael very often. Michael was the ultimate boss. There was no question about that, but there were many instances where he and I didn't agree—where I wouldn't back off and I keep dialoguing and ultimately either I was right or he was right and we reached the right conclusion and moved forward. I think it is a very dynamic thing; that is why I think I said earlier having respect for each other and having complementary skills is critically important.

AUTHORS: **Tell us more about the balance needed between shared and unique skills between the CEO and the COO.**

TOPFER: I think that if people are too similar in skills set, that could create a problem. As it turned out, Michael focused on the technology of the company;

he focused on the interfaces with the Street; he focused on the customer relationships because he did really well at that. He really had no interest in running the company on a day-to-day basis and getting very much involved in the operations and things like that. When I joined the company it was a $2.8 billion company and had never done a three-year plan and never did an annual plan, and it wasn't because they didn't want to do it. They just didn't have the structure and discipline to do it. In my first year at the company—1994—we did our first three-year plan.

AUTHORS: When you first got to Dell, what did you see as critical success issues for you in your new position?

TOPFER: There were many issues. One of the first issues we had to face was withdrawing from retail distribution. Not many people realize Dell was into that business early—also the first one out of it when we really decided we couldn't win at it. We actually made that decision before I joined the company. It was during a three-month transition when I was transitioning out of Motorola that I went to a few strategy sessions where we made that decision to get out of the retail business. But there were many challenges. The whole focus on quality that I was able to bring with me from Motorola had tremendous impact on Dell. Michael is very, very smart and listens very, very well. Together we really changed the whole momentum and direction of the company. The model that exists today Michael had already developed. It was really fine-tuning the model and bringing new dimension to it that I think worked very well. There weren't—I can't think of any issues where Michael and I went nose to nose on an issue. I don't think it is either of our style. We worked hard at bringing each other over to where we thought the right direction was but there were no . . . I don't think you can have very many knock-down, drag-out, you-win-or-I-win kind of situations and make it work. You have to be able to have conflict, but not let it become dysfunctional. The whole Dell culture was good at that. It was a very open, confrontational place, but once the decision was made, once we got down the direction decided upon, we executed flawlessly.

AUTHORS: Is there a time when a company needs a number two?

TOPFER: I grew up in Motorola. I spent twenty-three years there. They always had a two-in-a-box kind of structure. It always worked. It was something that

I was very comfortable with when I went to Dell. I frankly think that in today's world, with global businesses and so many challenges, I think it is impossible for a guy to run a company. There are some visible recent examples of CEO failure that result from one person trying to do the whole thing—to control everything through the office of the CEO. When you travel 70 percent of the time or whatever the number is, that has to lead to periods of indecision and people waiting for a decision and I just think those jobs are too big and complex and challenging for any normal human being to do it.

AUTHORS: Is there a life span for a number two?

TOPFER: Not necessarily. I was a number two for probably seven years. Given Michael's age and Kevin's age, I would guess Kevin is probably going to finish his career at Dell as the number two. When I say number two, he is the CEO but it still has Michael's name on the door. I think it is the same with Bill Gates at Microsoft. Ballmer has been CEO for a long time now, but I think Bill Gates is the father of Microsoft and always will be the "number one"—whatever his title. Those are tough situations; I think that is why number twos leave. I think they leave more often, like maybe in the GE case when Welch retired. One guy got the job and the other two people left to run great companies. You have to recognize that Michael is going to be there for the foreseeable future and you have to want it to be acceptable to live with that. I think it therefore says you can't be a very egocentric kind of guy like many CEOs are and really strive to have that title. It was not a big thing with Kevin.

AUTHORS: You mentioned the young, aggressive culture at Dell. Were there ever instances where you had to work hard at people not trying to work the two off against each other when trying to get a decision made?

TOPFER: I think that it became obvious very early in the game that doing so was kind of a death wish. We really knew what was going on, we communicated with each other. That was not a winning strategy at Dell.

A CONVERSATION WITH MAYNARD WEBB

COO, EBAY

As COO at eBay, Webb is responsible for coordinating companywide implementation of all business strategies. He joined eBay in 1999 as president, eBay Technologies. In that role, he was responsible for all engineering and technical operations at eBay, including product strategy, technology strategy, engineering, architecture, site operations, and customer support. Prior to joining eBay, Maynard was senior vice president and chief information officer at Gateway, a Fortune 250 leader in computing technology. He has also worked at Quantum, Thomas Conrad, Figgie International, and IBM (http://pages.ebay.com/aboutebay/thecompany/executiveteam.html#webb).

AUTHORS: Why do you think there are so many COOs in technology firms?

WEBB: In most technology companies, while there is a huge technology and sales/marketing component, generally there is also a huge operational component. I think it is really difficult to be all things to all people. Your top CEO in a technology firm is often not a sales/marketing person. For example, Larry Ellison is an engineering guy that needed Ray Lane, a COO with a sales/marketing background. Larry and Ray Lane were the reverse of what Meg and I have, where she fills the strategy and marketing roles, while I fill the operational and technical roles. The speed of the industry also plays a role; you are innovating, breaking new snow all the time. Your product cycles are such that if you miss a cycle, you are out of business.

AUTHORS: Can you share some key moments in your role as COO at eBay—episodes that really helped define the role?

WEBB: Probably the biggest impact thing I've been helping to drive over the time I've been COO is the people agenda of the company. We have a great strategy, we have great technology, and we have to ensure we have the managerial talent to fulfill our destiny. We have grown extraordinarily fast, which when combined with doing so in a new industry creates significant challenges.

Meg has joined me in leading this charge. Together we are working to define the kind of company we want this to be for our grandkids.

Taking the company from a small startup to a company with over ten thousand people has been challenging. In the beginning, we lacked process and continuity in areas such as setting objectives, focal reviews, and upward feedback. In creating the process, we met with some resistance. Now, that is all part of the ingrained culture. We had to get everybody behind the need to not only be great individual contributors but also great leaders and managers. In the end, the key thing was to bring discipline on the people front with transparency and consistency.

AUTHORS: A number of COOs who are the first to hold the position at a company have said that considerable time is spent trying to enforce the new reporting relationships—and that those accustomed to reporting directly to the CEO will spend a great deal of energy trying to find a back door to that office.

WEBB: That's been known to happen. I think it is a tough, tough thing. Especially when you have a CEO that likes to be involved in all facets of the business. I think what you have to do in this situation is enable—not control, be transparent, and then be strong enough to step up and do what is necessary. I will tell you, it is an art, not a science. It is a delicate balance.

I am the second COO at eBay. The first COO did not have the type of role that I have; he was a sales and marketing guy. In the early days, the three of us used to run eBay—Meg, Brian Swette (the first COO), and me. Brian ran the business units while I headed up technology. It was three in a box, if you will.

AUTHORS: You mentioned it is OK for the CEO and COO to take the gloves off behind closed doors and debate issues, but when out front, you stand shoulder-to shoulder.

WEBB: Yes, absolutely. Ninety-eight percent of the time it is shoulder-to-shoulder because there is true alignment. Managing the other 2 percent is really important. I think it's healthy to debate and question. It's critical that we play off of each other's strengths. However, you can't let little cracks become big fissures or it destroys the team. You will find executives who don't mind having fissures and deepening the divide. I don't think it's malicious, but a rebellion to being managed. It's certainly something we have to be aware of and watch for.

A CONVERSATION WITH WENDELL WEEKS

PRESIDENT AND CEO, CORNING

FORMERLY COO, CORNING

During his twenty-two-year career at Corning, Wendell Weeks has served in a range of manufacturing, product development, marketing, and executive positions. He originally joined the Controller's Division of Corning in 1983. Weeks was elected to the Corning board of directors in December 2000 and was appointed president and COO in April 2002. As COO, Weeks led Corning's restructuring and return to profitability following one of the most challenging periods in the company's 153-year history. In January 2005, Corning announced that Weeks would become the company's president and chief executive officer, effective in April 2005 (http://www.corning.com/inside_corning/corporate_governance/our_leadership/WWeeks.aspx).

AUTHORS: What does it take for somebody to be successful in the COO role?

WEEKS: There are a variety of skills that you need to be a successful senior executive. One of the things that makes the COO job different is the relationship and the ability to partner with your CEO, as well as the other senior executives who don't work directly for you but also report to the CEO. Because we are in so many businesses, a broad range of pre-COO experiences is important. We are in telecom, display, environmental, automotive.

AUTHORS: Please talk a little bit more about the unique relationship that the COO has to form with the CEO.

WEEKS: Let me use an example. I have a strong right hand, from an operations standpoint, working for me. He used to run half the company. I used to run half the company. Now he works for me. If I were to become a CEO, he would be my first choice as COO, far and away. He and I actually went through a very similar type of relationship to that of a CEO-COO. We actually sat down and described our partnership principles. "Here is how we are going to operate as partners," not as me as boss, him as supervisee. But rather true partners.

I did not do that same formal process with our then-CEO, Jamie Houghton; much more was left unsaid. Jamie did say that in his approach as a returning CEO he wasn't going to be highly engaged in the detailed steering of the company. He is going to make sure we live our values. He is going to work the board, make sure he has the leadership team that he wants; but the strategic decision making and the "what we have to do when," that is much more left to the other members of the management committee. That was his approach to the role. Every CEO approaches the role differently.

The key thing that will derail a COO one way or another is mostly perceptual. If the CEO makes the COO appear "less" in any way, the partnership is not going to work. When I was COO, if the CEO were to dominate me or overmanage me, then that would not work. The idea of it being a true partnership in every sense of the word really is a critical thing that has worked for us.

A partnership between the CEO and COO works great. When it works, you wouldn't trade it. I would not trade it for having a true boss-subordinate relationship, because I have had plenty of those—you know, you can't get to my current job without that. But I wouldn't trade it. If you can get a real partner, that is better. And your odds of making a mistake are less and your odds of seeing opportunity are more.

6

CONCLUSION

The man who occupies the first place seldom plays the
principal part.
        Johann Wolfgang von Goethe, The Sorrows of Werther

There are few decisions as critical to an organization as those involving how
its leadership team is structured. Our goal has been to promote a better understanding of the nuances associated with one such structure, that involving
the designation of a clear second in command. Though announcements of
COO comings and goings appear daily in the business press, there has previously not been much of an effort to understand what might cause a firm to
implement this structure successfully. As we noted at the outset, the mixed
experiences firms have had from implementing the role, combined with the
relative lack of attention the role has received, caused us to undertake this effort. From our interviews, we have been able to identify a number of points
that we think can offer guidance to boards, CEOs, and COO incumbents and
candidates, as well as consultants and academics interested in the role and its
impact, to better know how to successfully plan and execute the decision to
create a COO position.

CONSIDERATIONS FOR BOARDS AND CEOS

A consistent and important piece of advice that our executives shared is that
CEOs have to be confident that they understand what they need to invest if
they are to honor their commitment to the success of the COO. If the COO
comes from outside the firm or if the COO is not someone with whom the
CEO has an existing relationship, the time necessary to assess fit, bring on
board, and develop a productive relationship can be enormous. Of course, the

organization does not stand still while this process unfolds, creating additional demands on the CEO's time.

Certainly, a part of the CEO's resolution to create a COO position should be based on a sound business case. We identified seven motivations on which a firm could build such a case: to impart daily leadership in an operationally intensive business, carry out leadership for a specific strategic initiative, mentor an inexperienced CEO, balance the strengths of the CEO, create a strong partnership, learn the business as heir, and retain talent. We suggest that wide communication of the business case for the position be a priority. All key constituents—the board, the CEO, the top management team, and so on—should share an understanding of why the position is being created. From that understanding come indications of the measures on which the success or failure of the position can be based. That said, it was stressed to us that the position is by its nature amorphous and that firms need to design the role and its relationships with other members of top management around the personalities involved, as well as the company's needs.

Steve Kerr, now at Goldman Sachs, shared with us an insight he gleaned from his time at GE as chief learning officer under Jack Welch. In essence, he told us that Welch had a concern that too many layers of management acted like sweaters for a CEO. At some point, you end up wearing so many sweaters that you can no longer tell if it is cold outside; you lose touch with your environment. Our interviews acknowledged that, although the COO could lend a second set of hands on deck, it is important that the CEO not let the position end up being a sweater that prevents him or her from understanding where the business is. In fact, we saw instances where new CEOs eliminated, at least for a time, a COO position for precisely this reason.

If it had not been clear before our interviews, it quickly became evident that the quality of the relationship between the CEO and COO is critical. The fit between the two individuals needs to be assessed on a number of dimensions. As we described, the importance of each dimension varies with the motivation behind the creation of the role. In some instances, complementary skill sets will be the most important consideration. Such is the case in creating a two-in-a-box leadership model. At other times, in leadership succession, for example, simple demographics such as the age difference become important. Probably one of the most important things on which the CEO and COO must agree concerns the career aspirations of the COO and the degree to which they may or may not be accommodated by the firm. More than one of our executives suggested that CEOs watch out for overly ambitious COOs. The concern here is not necessarily that such a person would deliberately put self-interest over the interests of the firm, but instead that it is impossible to do the COO job if the incumbent's eyes are on the desired next job. A disagreement between the CEO and the COO over the likelihood and timing of a succession is arguably the most damaging sort of misalignment that can occur between the two; in this instance, both executives are at risk of derailment.

Finally, our respondents went to great lengths to detail the critical nature of the assimilation process for COOs. The process begins during recruiting and continues for some time after the COO joins the firm. Of particular importance are a shared understanding of the four corners, or boundaries, of the job, both at the outset and as things evolve; CEO investment in building a trusting relationship characterized by open communication and a shared public front; and consistent consensus from each executive as to the other's decision-making authority. In addition, it is a great benefit for the COO when the CEO is persistent, deliberate, and obvious about creating opportunities for the COO to interact meaningfully with the board and other key constituents. In some instances, the involvement of the COO is deemed important enough to warrant a seat on the board. In any form, board involvement is important as a developmental opportunity for the COO. This should occur whether or not the COO has been identified as the heir apparent because of the role such interaction plays in reinforcing the authority vested in the COO. Lack of this involvement is another potential contributor to failure of the CEO-COO structure to produce sought-after results.

CONSIDERATIONS FOR COOS AND COO CANDIDATES

Of course, the considerations for boards and CEOs that have been summarized here also afford some insight to COOs and COO candidates. That aside, our interviews furnish some commentary that it is important to highlight specifically for this group. First of all, the COOs we interviewed were unanimous in their opinion that the job is a relentless one. As one seasoned COO explained, it isn't just a matter of (to use Jim Collins's metaphor) "getting the right people on the bus." It is a matter of getting the right people on the bus while the bus careens down the highway at a high rate of speed. The bus never finishes its trip—and the people you need on the bus frequently change.

As far as the specific details surrounding a particular COO position, there was similar unanimity as to the importance of a sense that the person serving as CEO be absolutely excellent. If a COO harbors any doubt about the quality of the CEO, many things can happen; none of them, short of the removal of the CEO, are of much benefit to organizational stakeholders. If a COO candidate does not think the CEO is top caliber, he or she should stay away from the position. Taking the point a bit further, the COO should also try to anticipate how long he or she would be able to serve under the CEO. As noted, even the strongest mentor-protégé relationships have natural a life span. The key question to ask is whether or not the opportunity is a good one, given career aspirations of the COO, the amount of runway likely left in the CEO's tenure, and the organization's succession plans. Finally, as we have noted, the candidate should be confident that the CEO will allow the COO to have his or her own voice and be more than a transactional leader in the firm. Absent those two important job characteristics, the position does not set someone up very well to move to a CEO opportunity.

A related consideration concerns the nature of the interpersonal relationships among the members of the top management team. It is particularly important for outside candidates to try to ascertain this. If the candidate is filling a position that has created a major structural change for the organization—or if the position has resulted in major shifts in reporting lines and duties of other top managers—the perceived ability to quickly develop productive relationships with these other managers becomes important. To the extent the COO position creates what these managers might see as problems, such as a barrier to CEO access and so on, doing so will be difficult. Being able to quickly size up the political landscape among the top management team is a capability that will serve an incoming COO quite well.

Finally, our respondents differed with regard to their sense of how well experience as a COO prepares someone to serve as CEO. This is not surprising given the variation in how the job is structured. Certainly some COOs are exposed to many, if not all, of the key elements of the CEO job, whereas others serve in a more narrowly defined, more strictly operational role. What the respondents did agree on, however, is the importance for COOs to do an honest self-assessment of their capabilities so they can understand in advance what deficiencies might exist. Ideally, COOs with aspirations for a higher position would engage in such a process continuously through their time as COO, lobbying for opportunities to broaden their experience and improve their preparation. There is no doubt that a board evaluating potential successors would want to be sensitive to the degree to which COOs have experience in the areas most often viewed as hard to imitate in a COO role: managing relationships with the board, speaking to the Street, and making difficult decisions understanding that the responsibility for the decision and its outcomes now belongs to them.

CONSIDERATIONS FOR FURTHER STUDY

As noted at the outset, one of our goals for this undertaking was to encourage insights that might be used to inform further study of the COO role and the CEO-COO leadership structure. The most important observation gleaned from the interviews is that the role escapes a single definition, except in the broadest sense as the number two executive. As a result, efforts to study the role need to begin with appreciation of the situational contingencies that apply. Rather than asking if the CEO-COO structure is an effective way to lead a firm, the question should be, "In what situations is the structure an effective way to lead a firm?" Among the most important contingencies to model are:

- The firm's motivations for creating the position
- The nature and quality of the interpersonal relationship between the CEO and COO
- The nature and quality of the relationships between the COO and other members of the top management team
- The nature and quality of the relationship between the COO and the board
- The thoroughness and accuracy of the prehire due diligence conducted by the firm and the COO candidate
- The success of the CEO and other members of top management in executing the process of bringing the COO on board.

In all, our contention is that the effectiveness of both the CEO-COO structure and the COO as an individual should be thought of as the product of a multidimensional fit that includes "executive fit" between the COO and the CEO (e.g., with regard to skills, trust, and personal relations), "person-job fit" (e.g., the capabilities of the COO with regard to the motivation for creating the position), and "person-opportunity fit" (e.g., a match between the firm's succession plans and COO aspirations). By starting with an assessment of the degree to which a firm has created fit, efforts to understand the impact of the role on subsequent firm performance will be strengthened.

INDEX